Lets Draw Together: A Fun and Easy Guide for Young Artist

Thank You for your purchase.

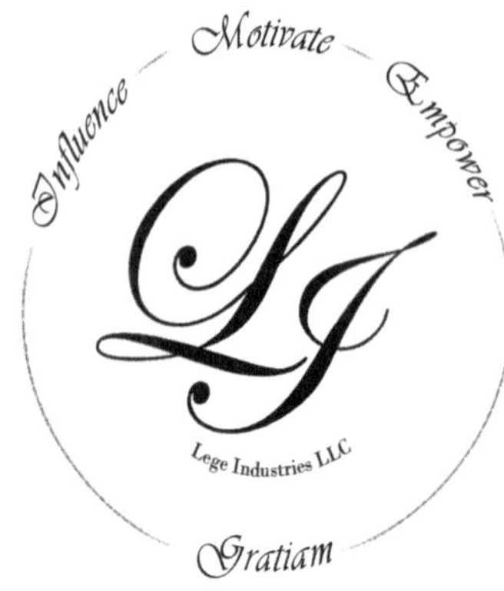

Check out other great books like this one by visiting us at:

https://legeindustriesllc.com

Or scanning the QR code below

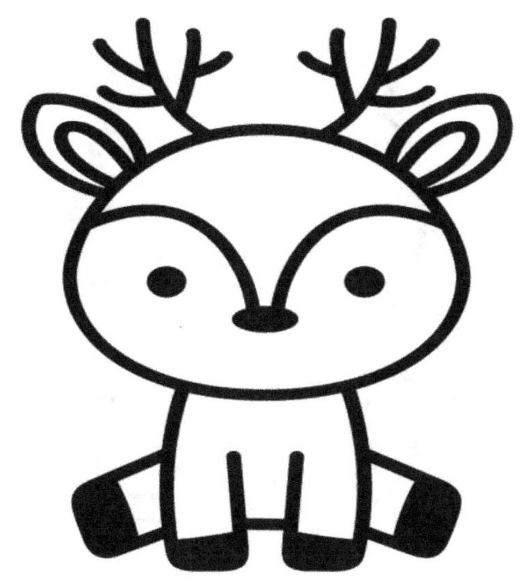

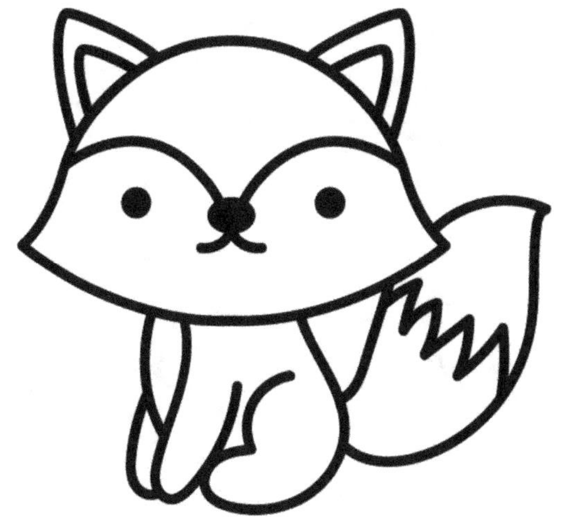

THIS BOOK BELONGS TO:

____

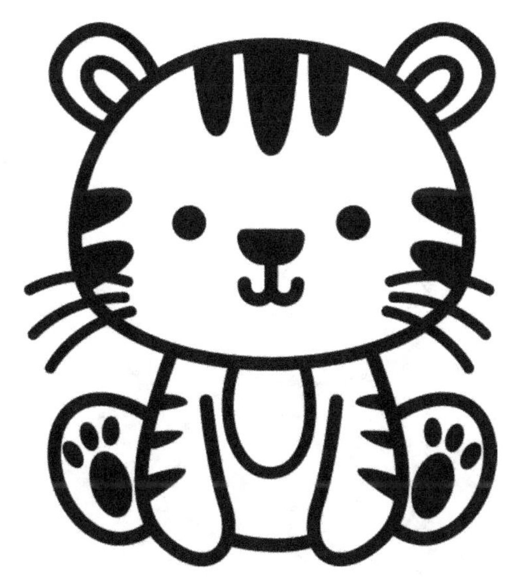

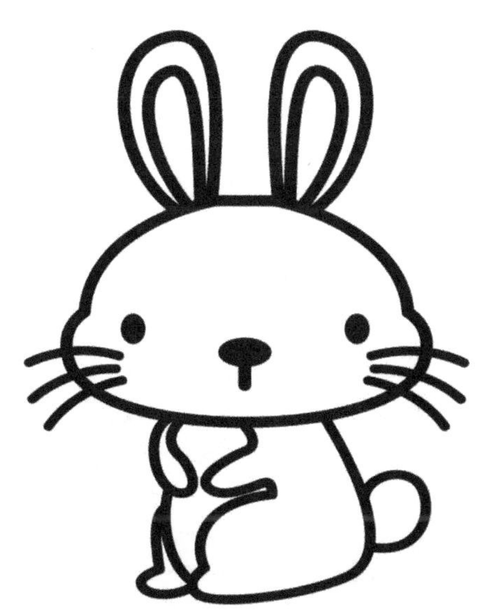

Thank You

Influence
Motivate
Empower
LJ
Lege Industries LLC
Gratiam

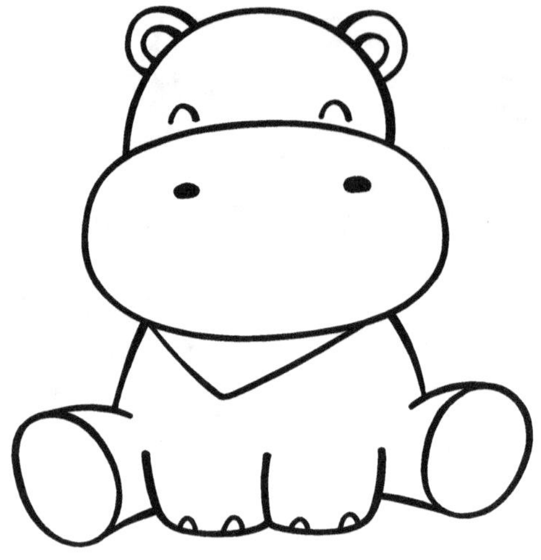

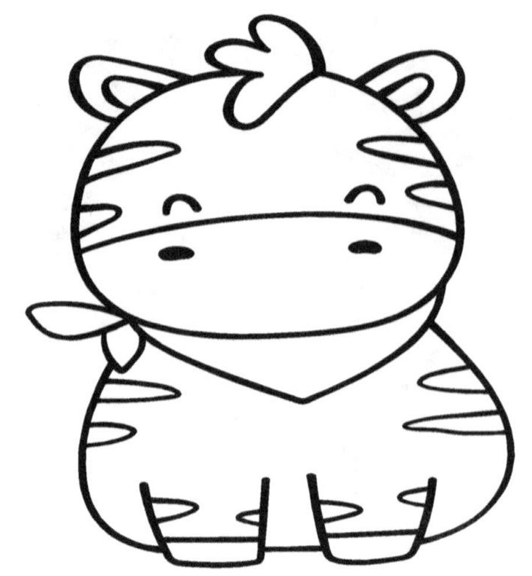

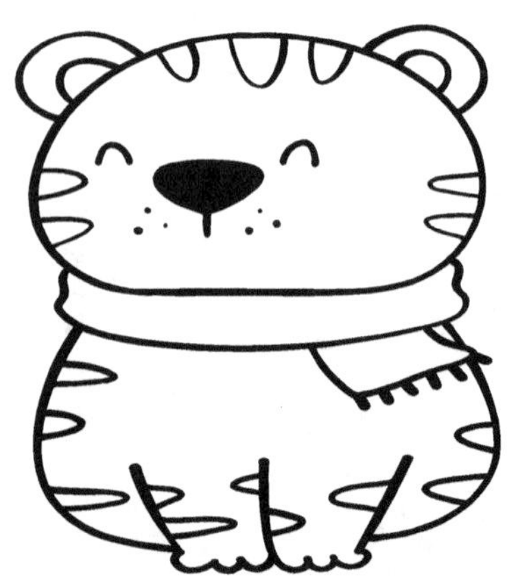

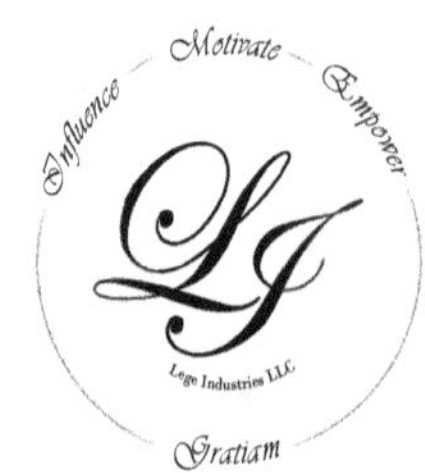

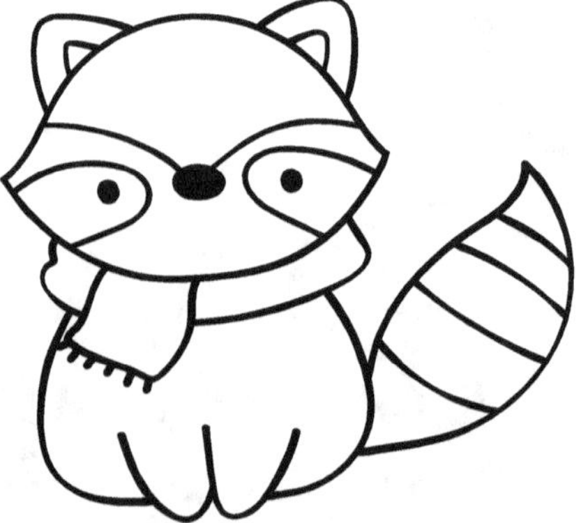

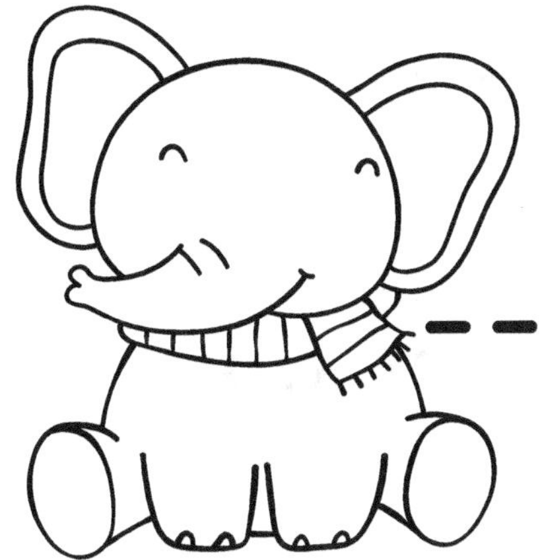

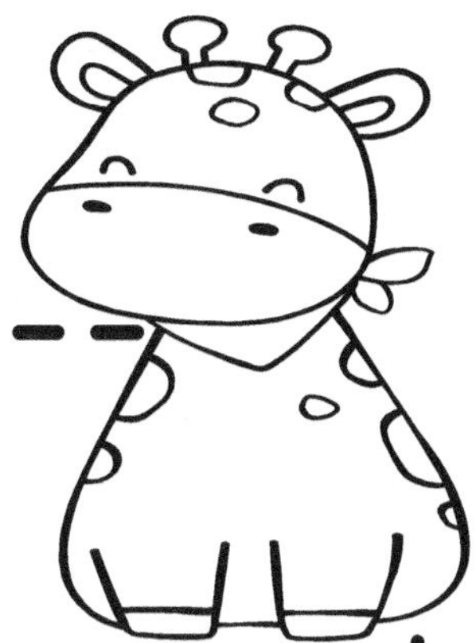

How to Use This Book

- Prepare a pencil and eraser. You can use pens, markers or any tool you like.
- Start by drawing lightly so that it can be easily erased if there are mistakes.
- Continue by following the numbers.
- If you get stuck, refer to the final drawing.
- You can color what you drew.

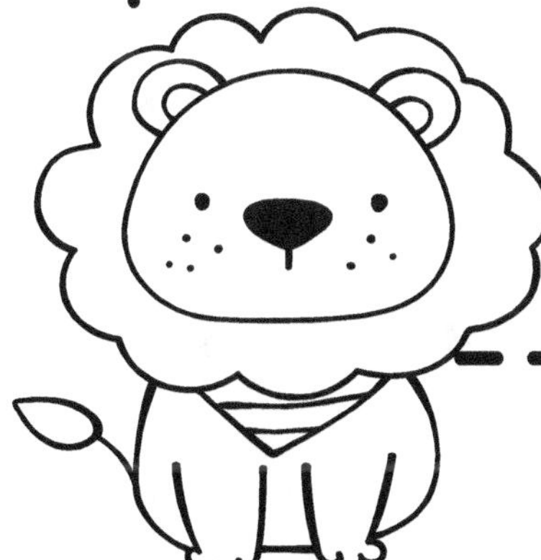

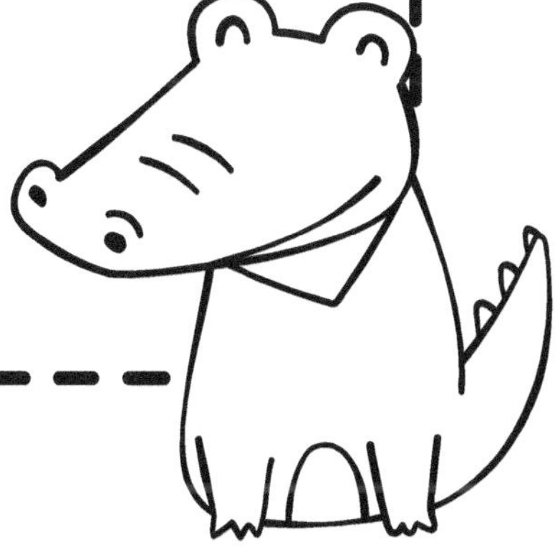

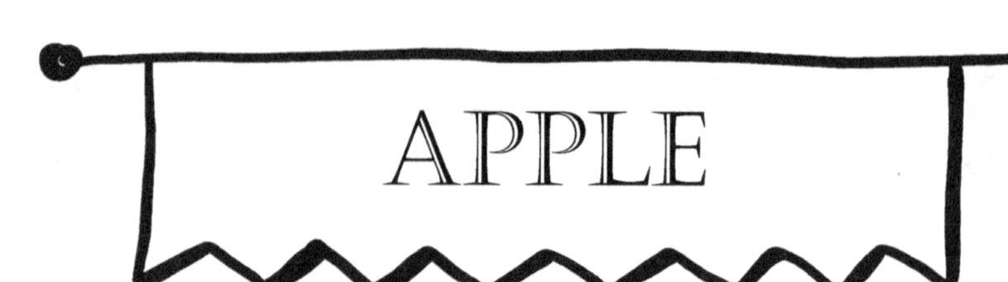

Step 1

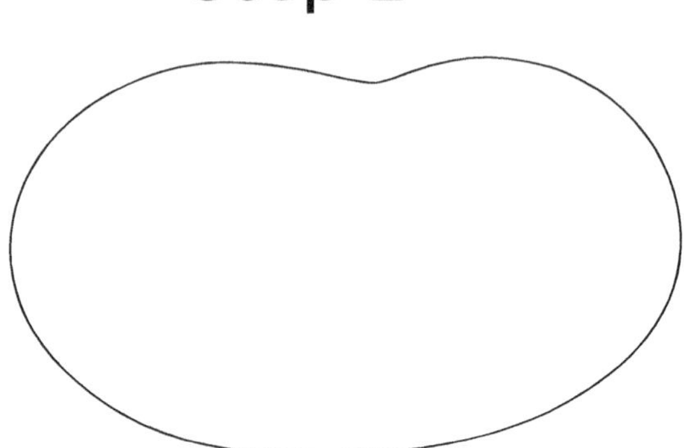

Step 2

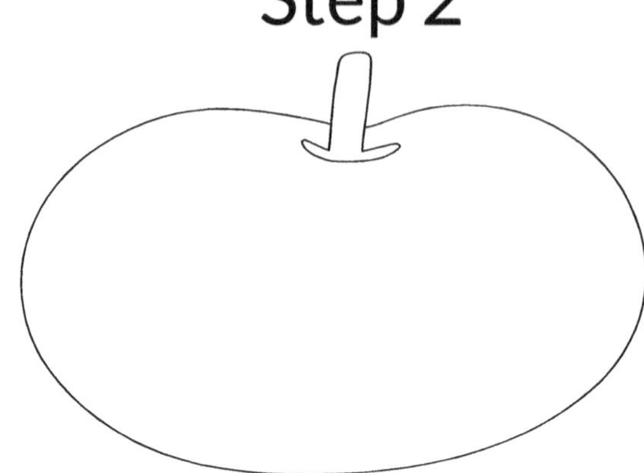

Step 3

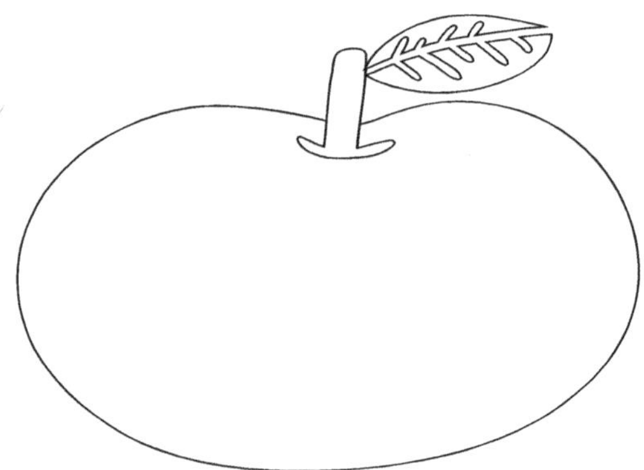

Step 4

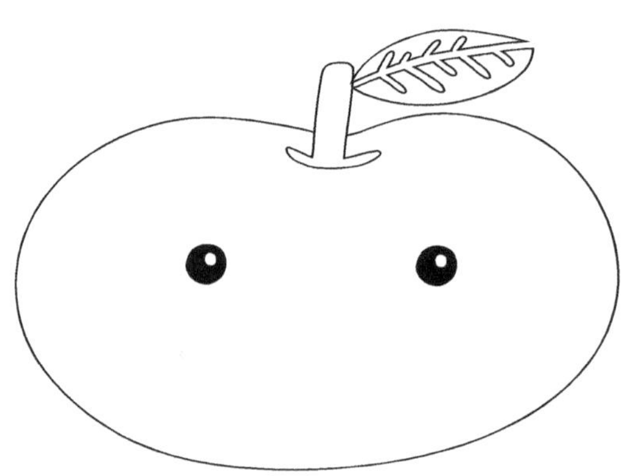

Step 5

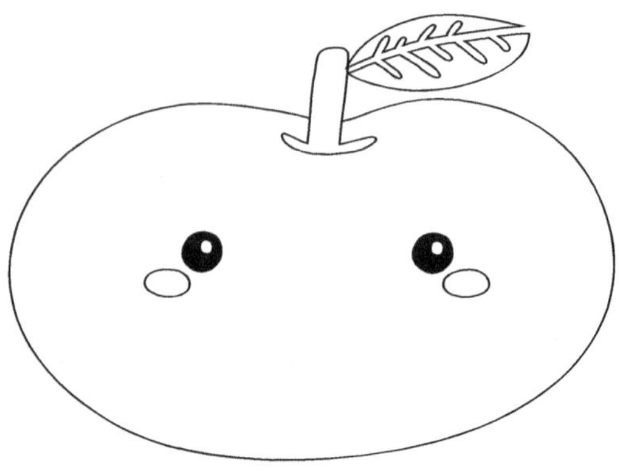

Step 6

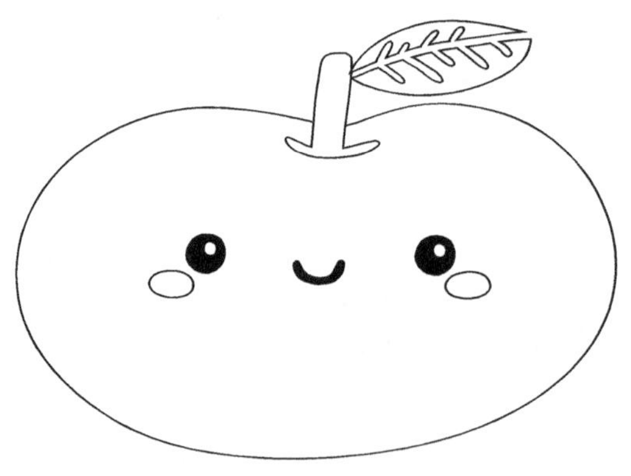

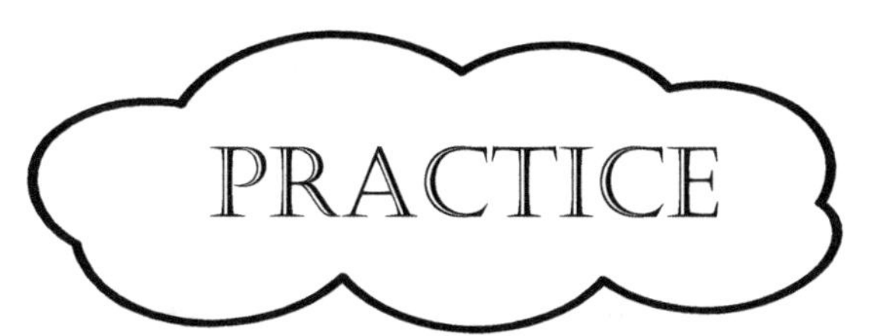
PRACTICE

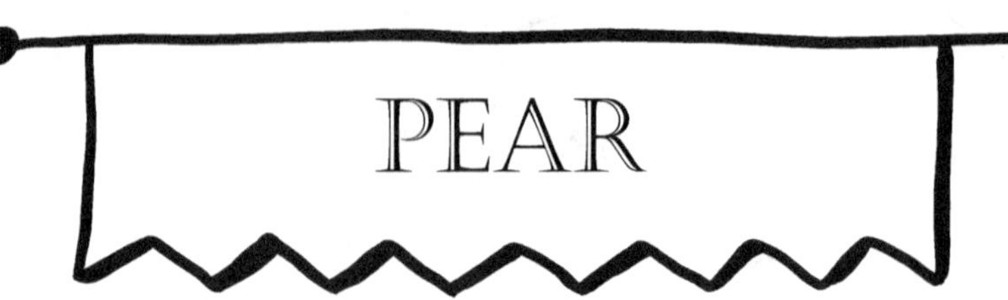

Step 1

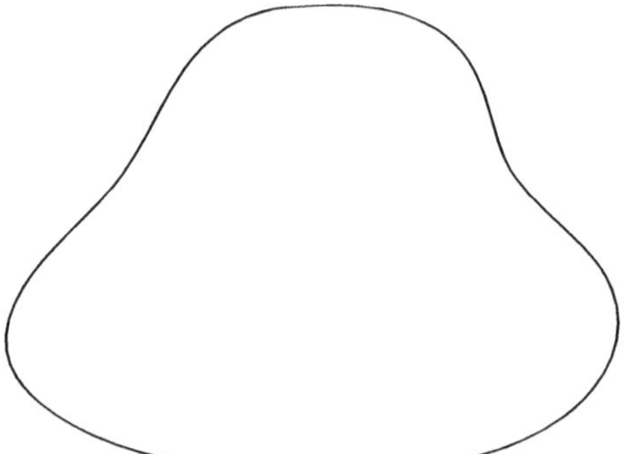

Step 2

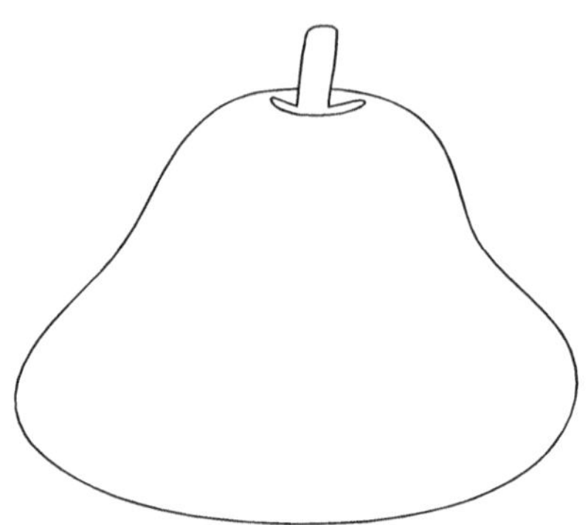

Step 3

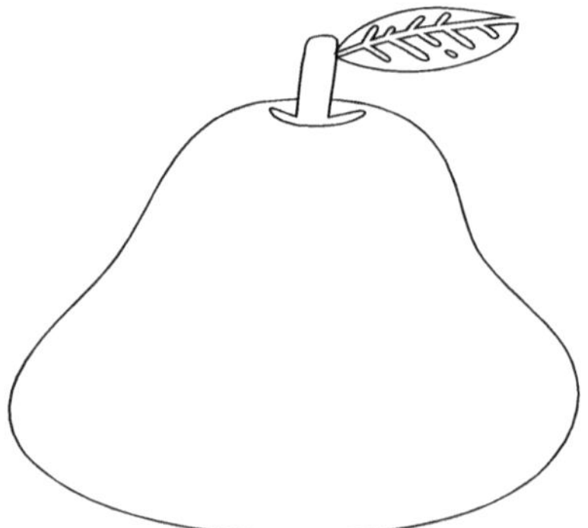

Step 4

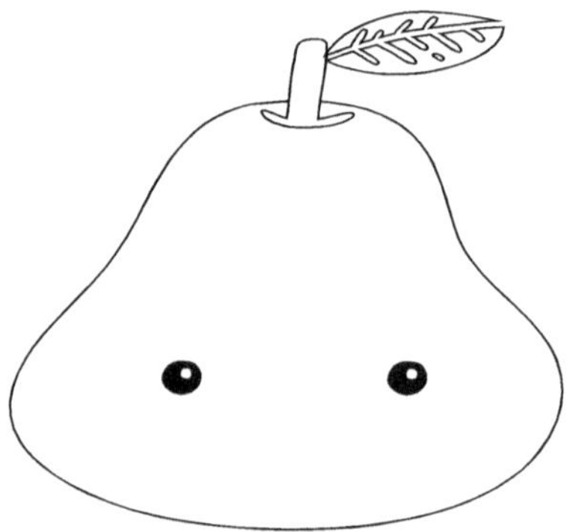

Step 5

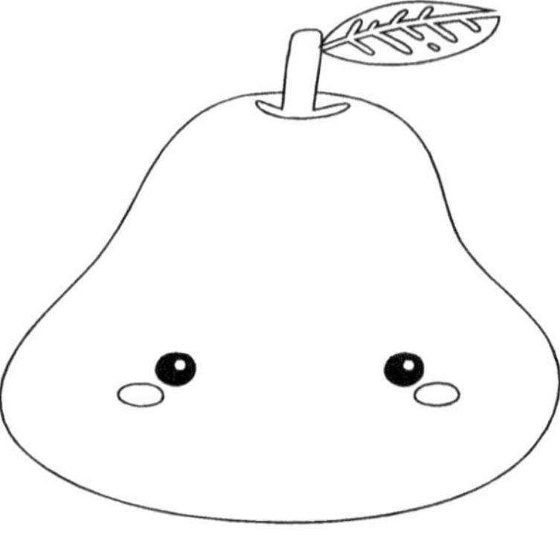

Step 6

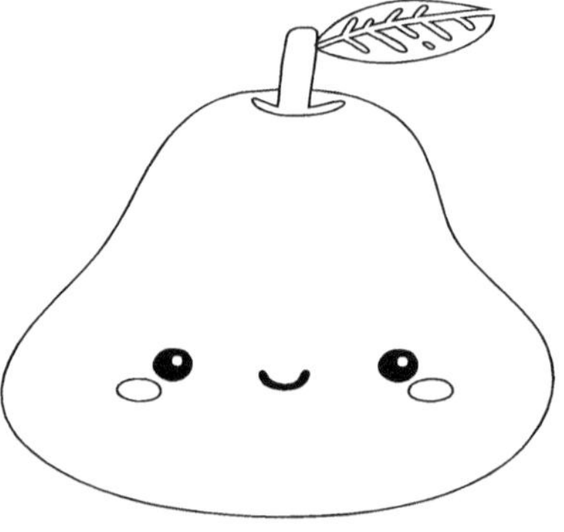

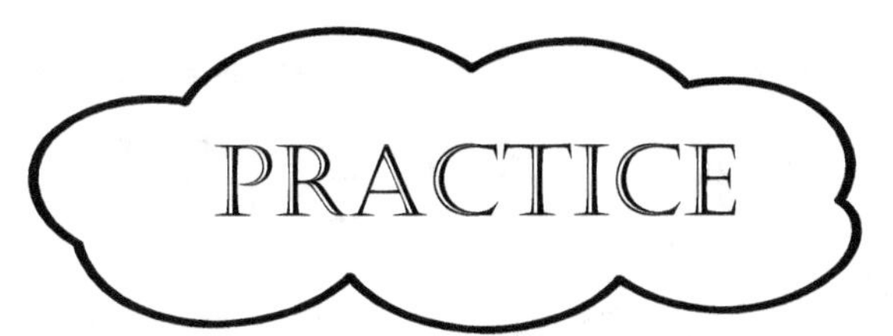
PRACTICE

STRAWBERRY

Step 1

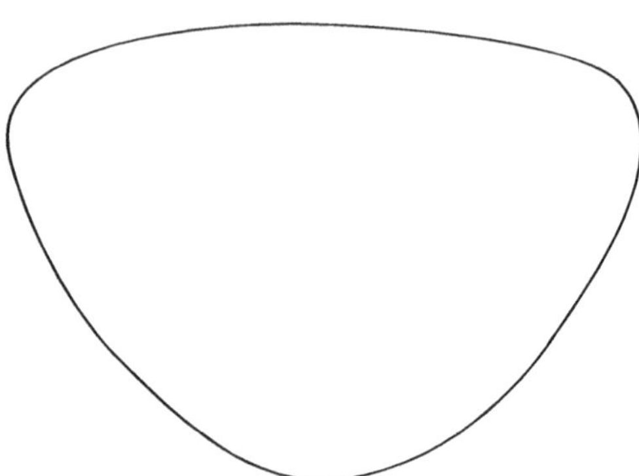

Step 2

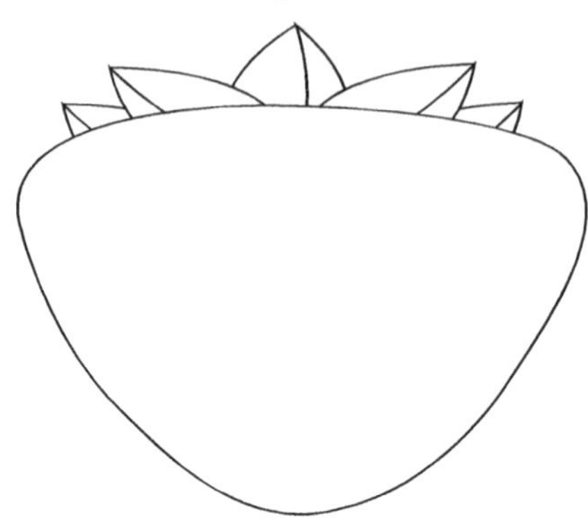

Step 3

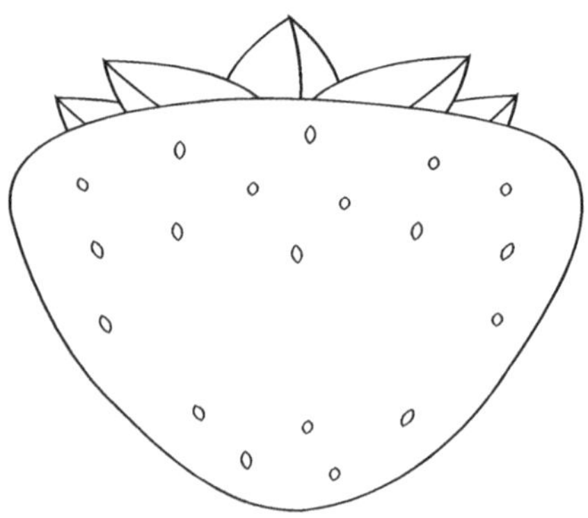

Step 4

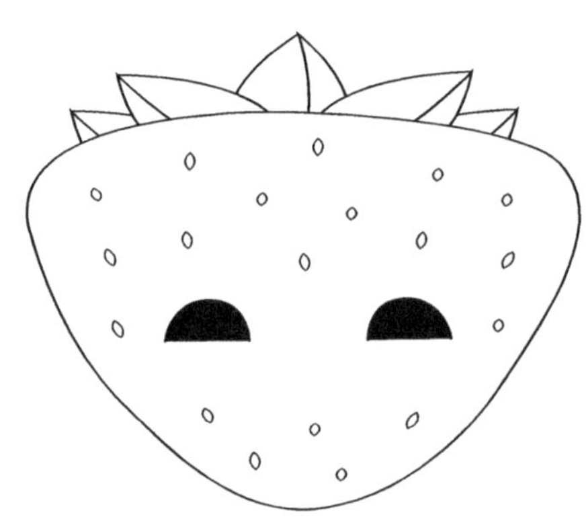

Step 5

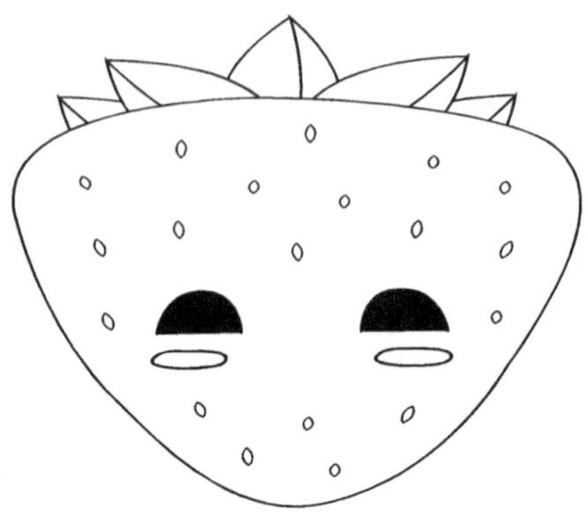

Step 6

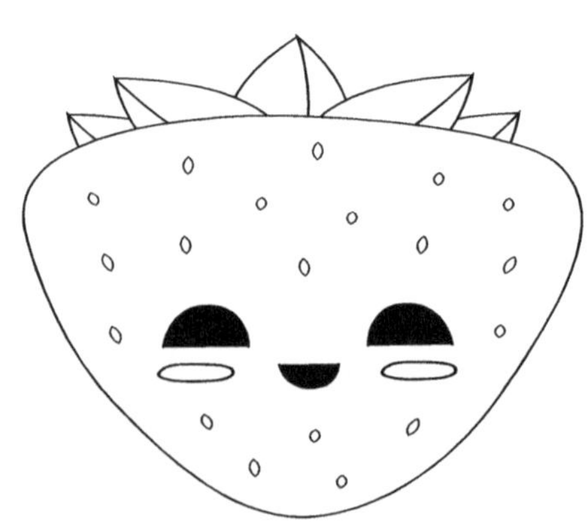

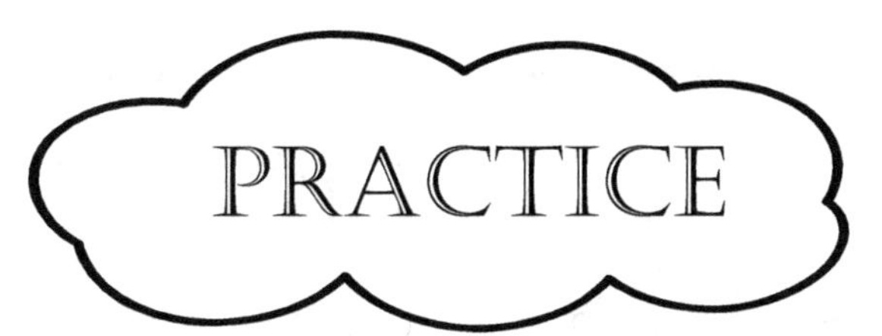
PRACTICE

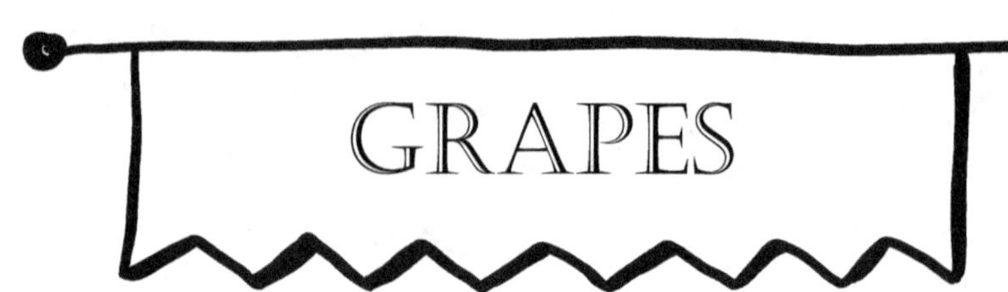

Step 1

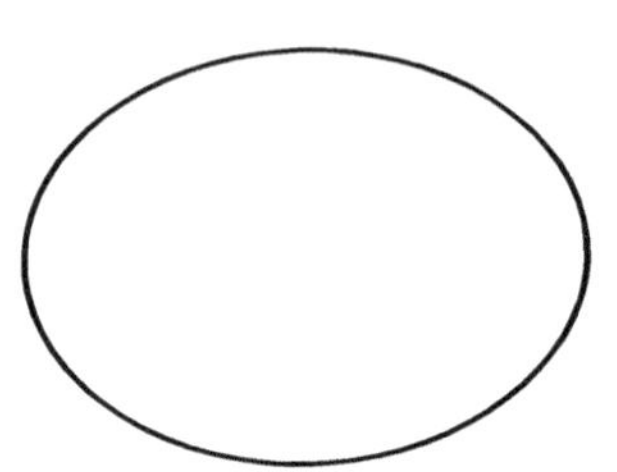

Step 2

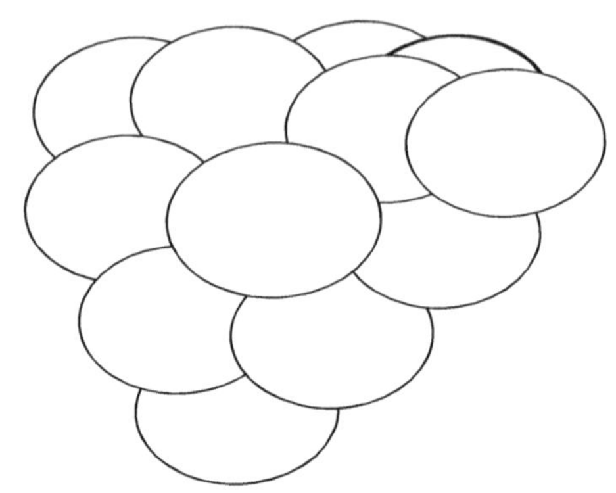

Step 3

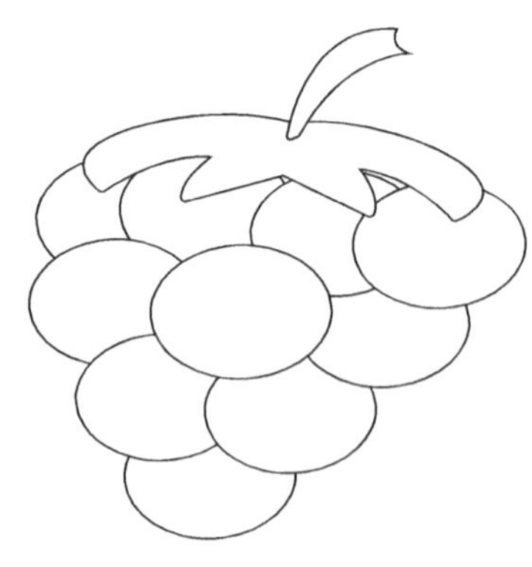

Step 4

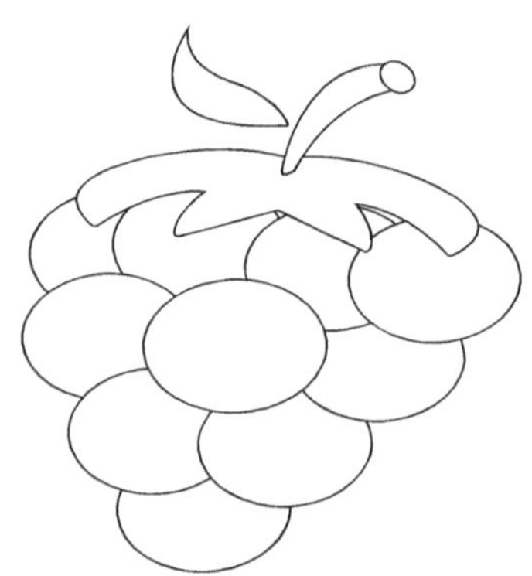

Step 5

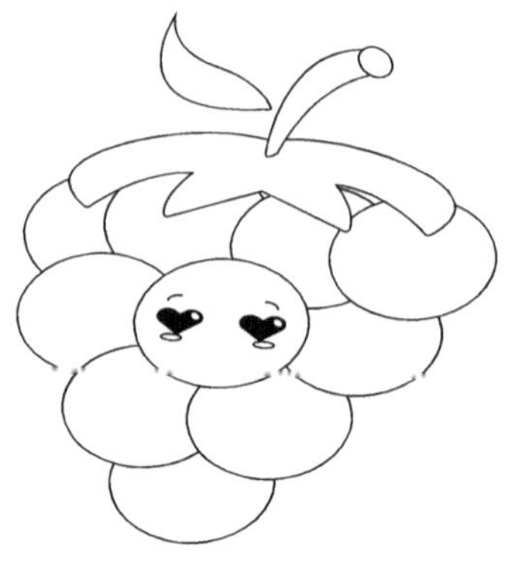

Step 6

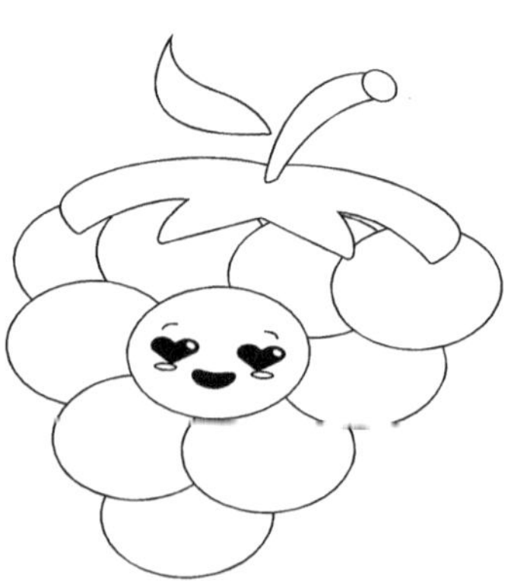

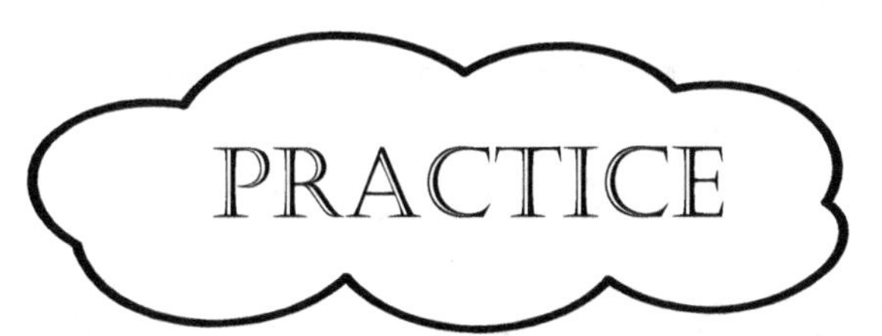
PRACTICE

LEMON

Step 1

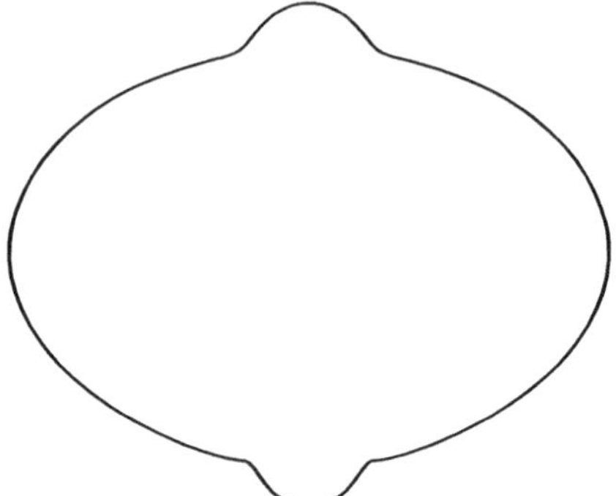

Step 2

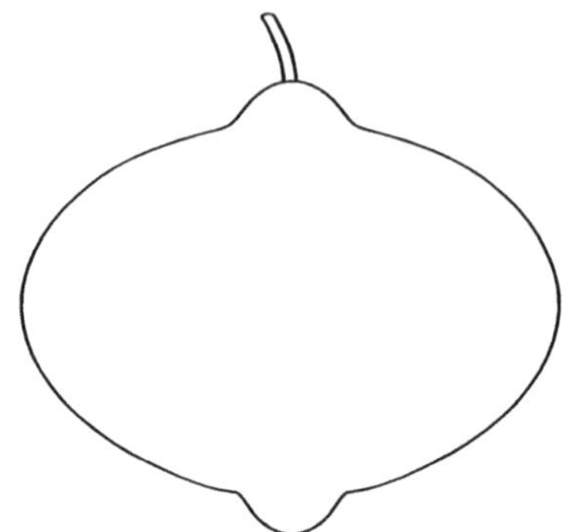

Step 3

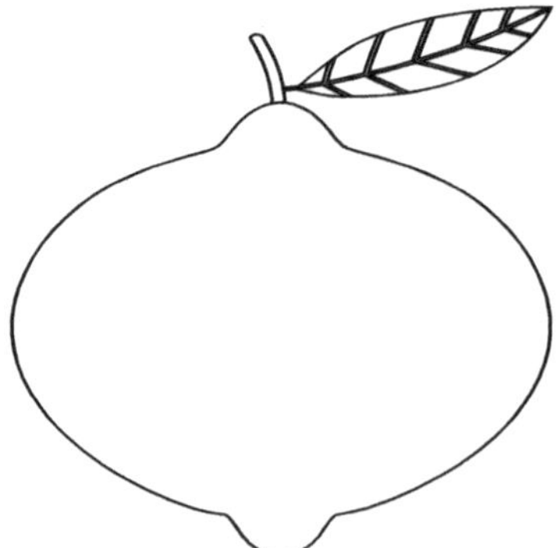

Step 4

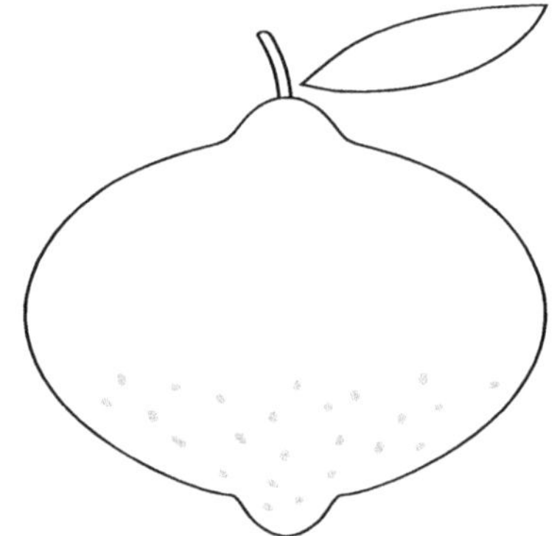

Step 5

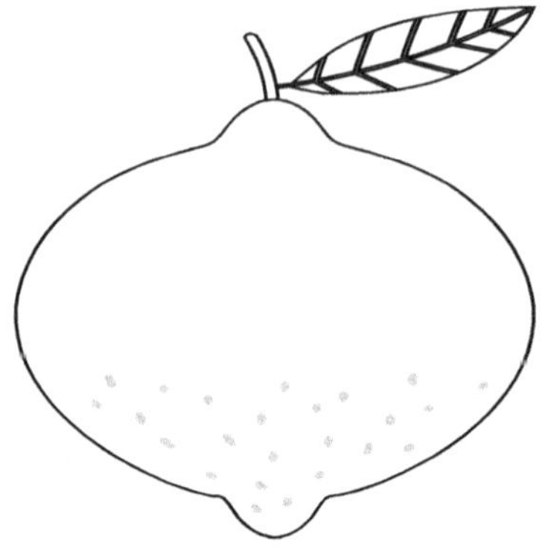

Step 6

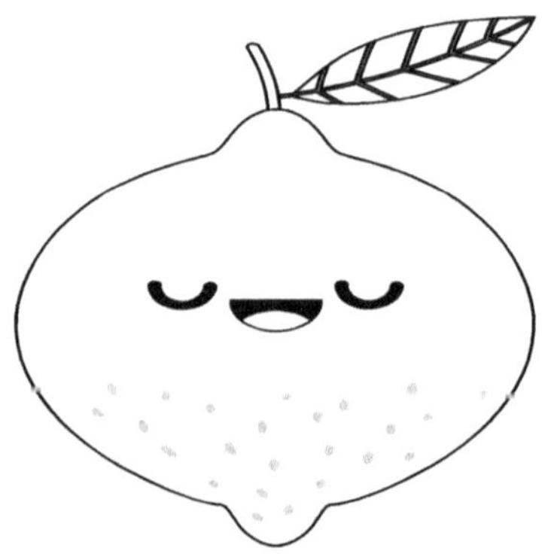

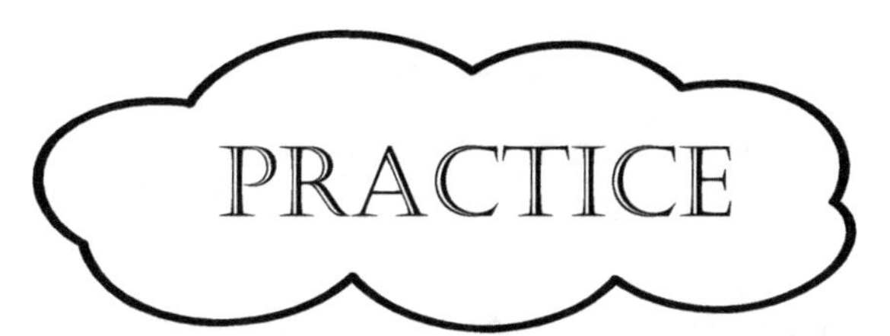
PRACTICE

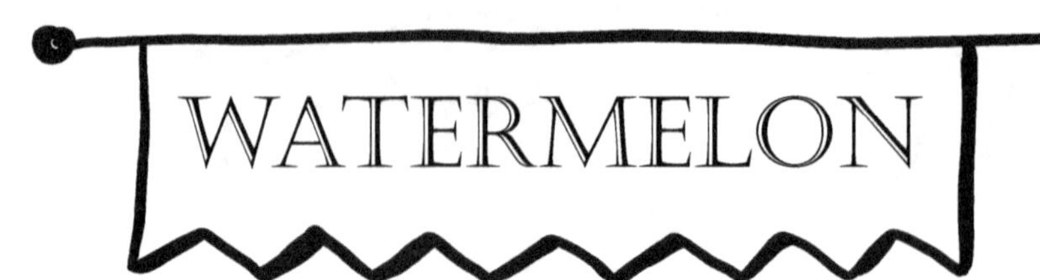

Step 1

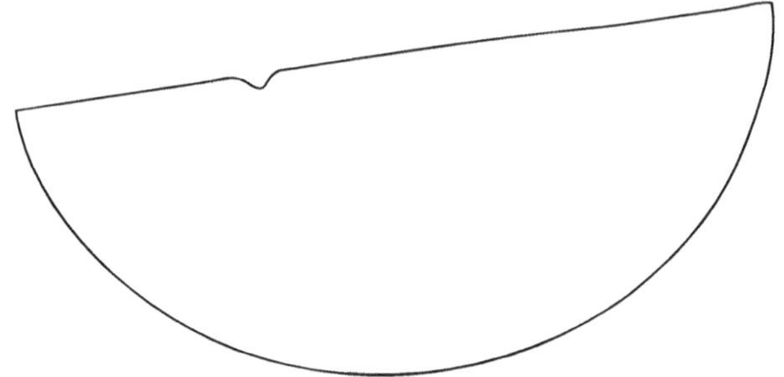

Step 2

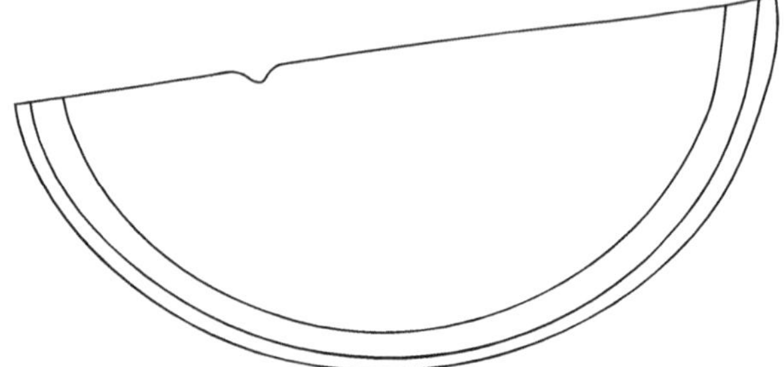

Step 3

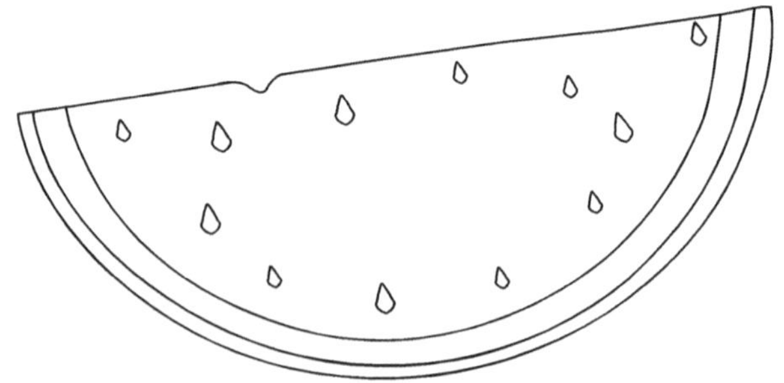

Step 4

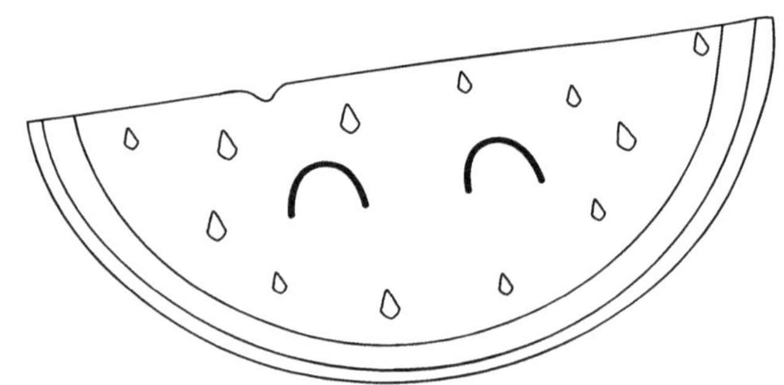

Step 5

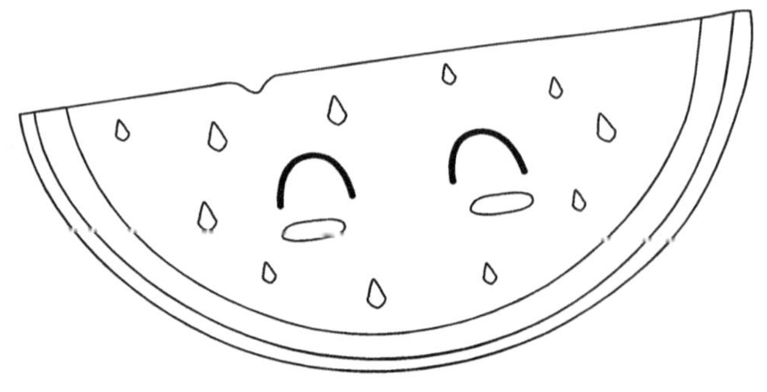

Step 6

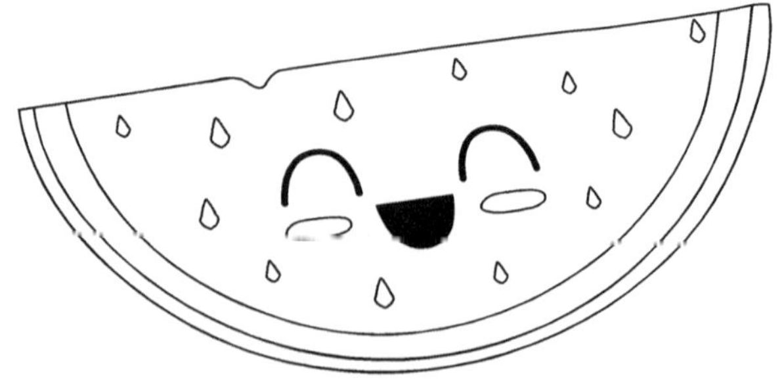

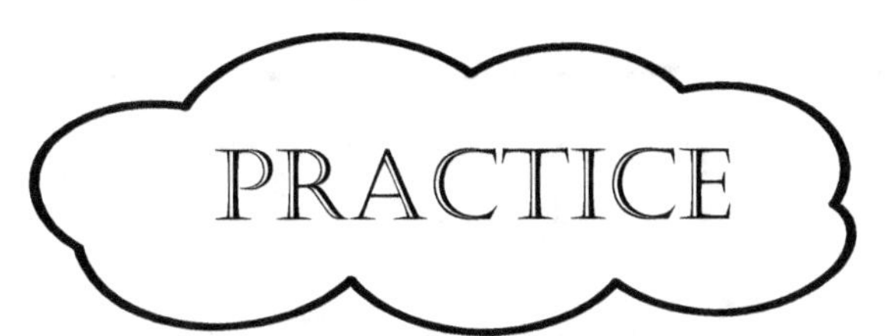
PRACTICE

TOMATO

Step 1

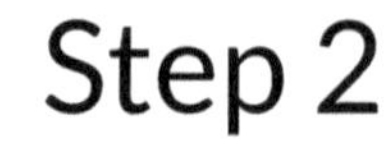

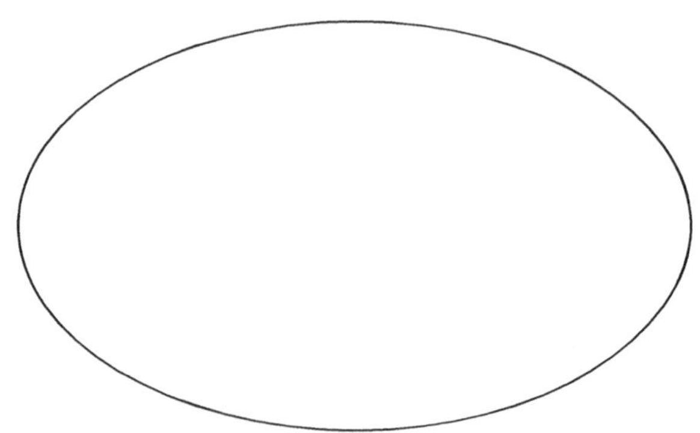

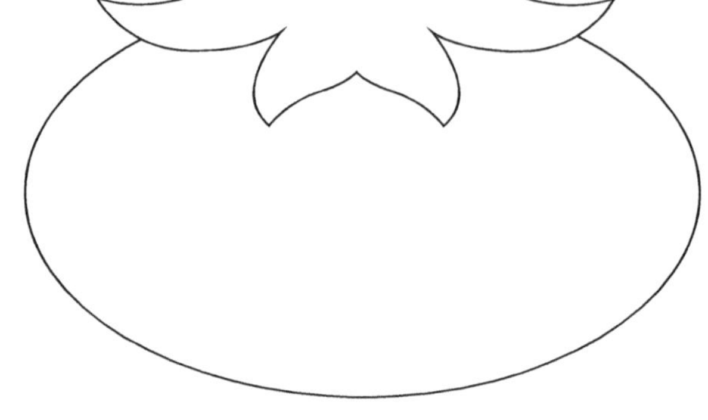

Step 3

Step 4

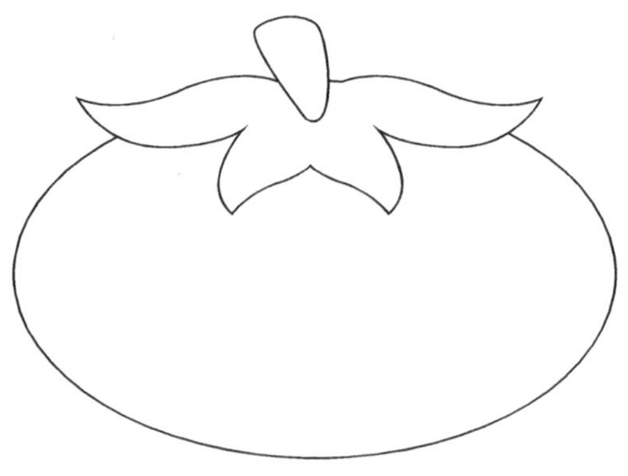

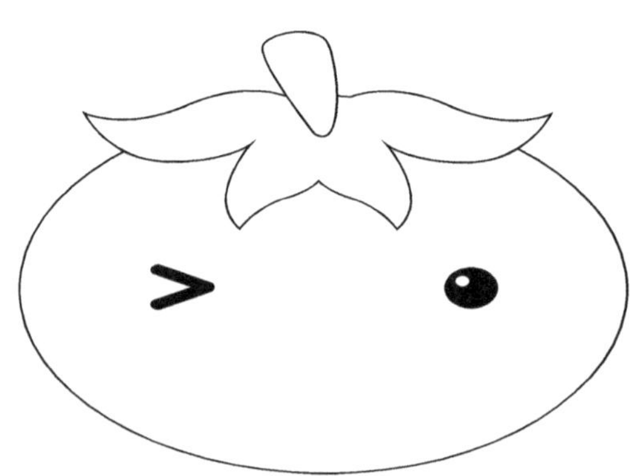

Step 5

Step 6

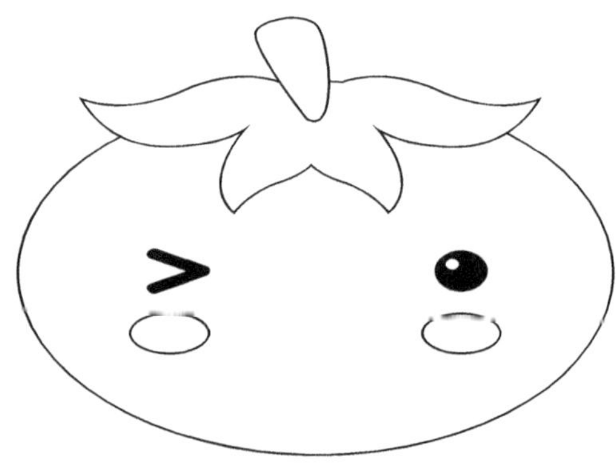

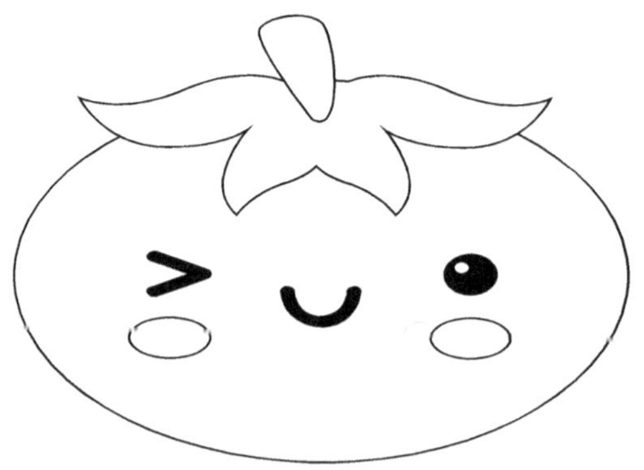

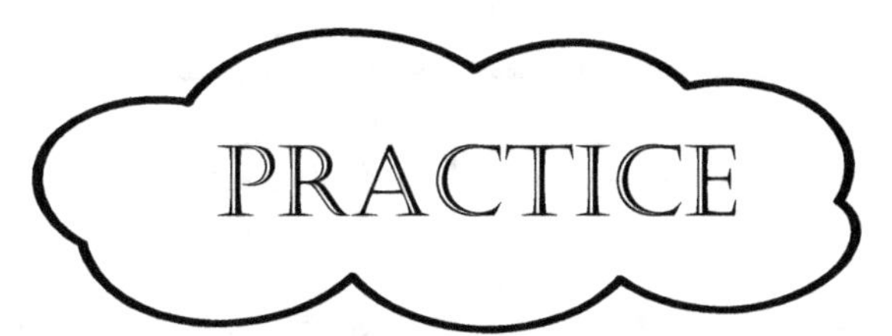
PRACTICE

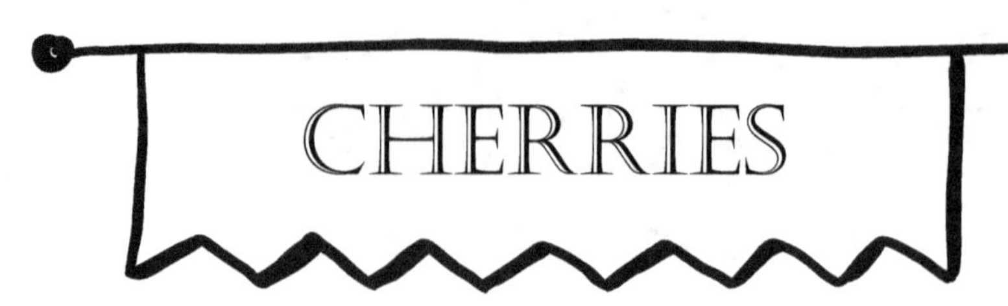

Step 1

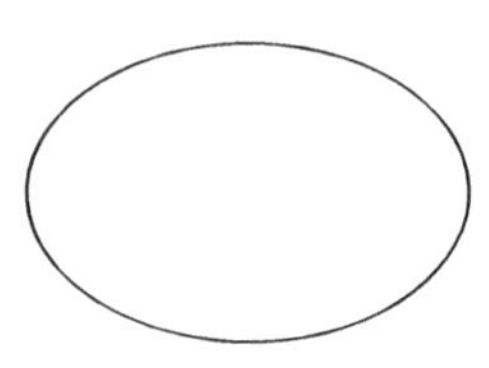

Step 2

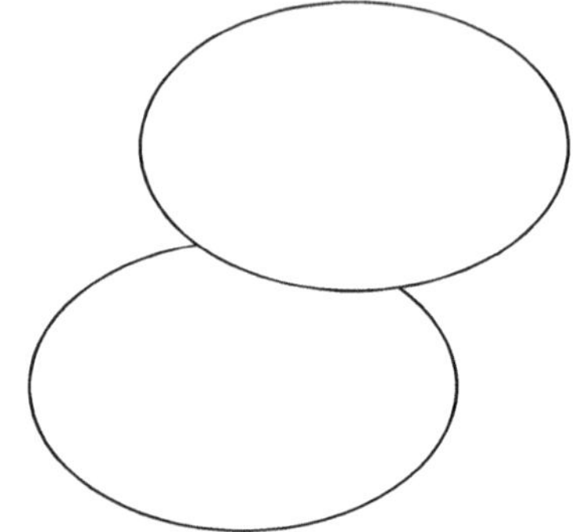

Step 3

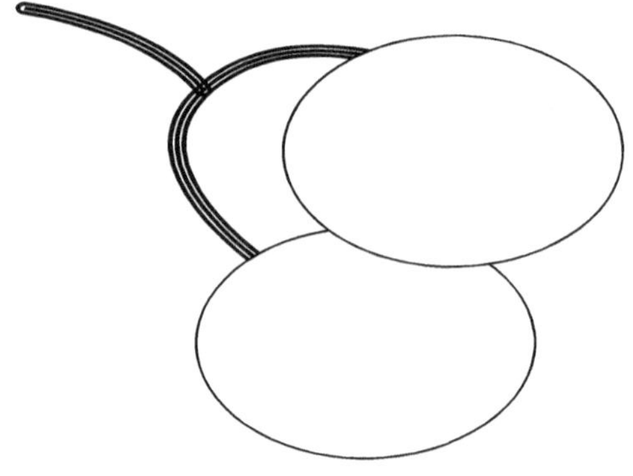

Step 4

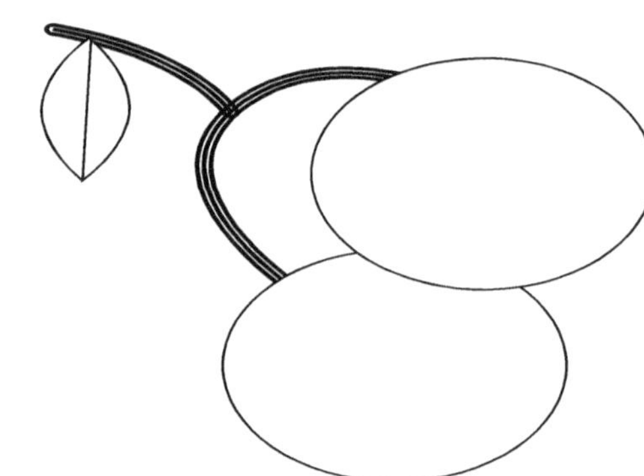

Step 5

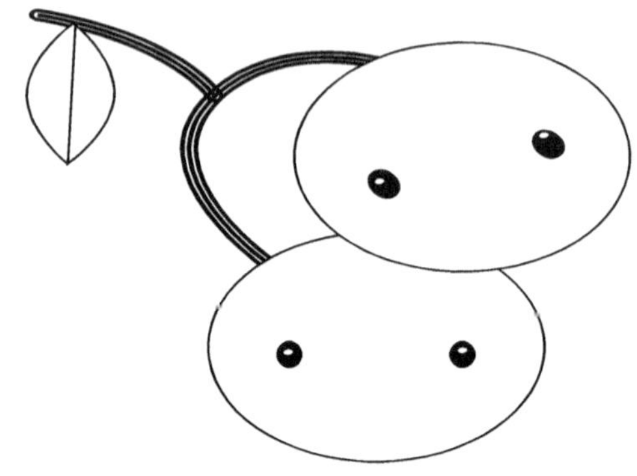

Step 6

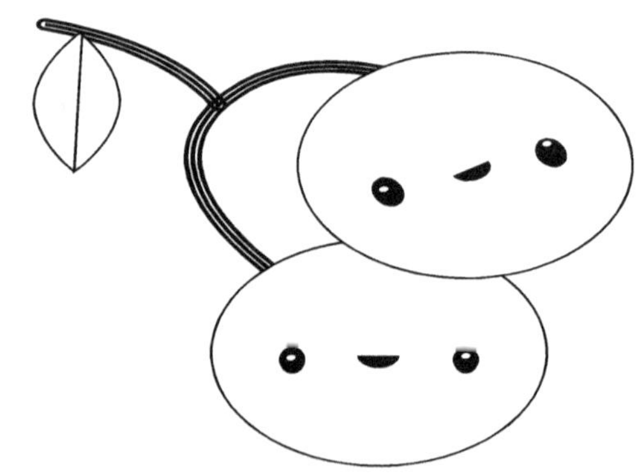

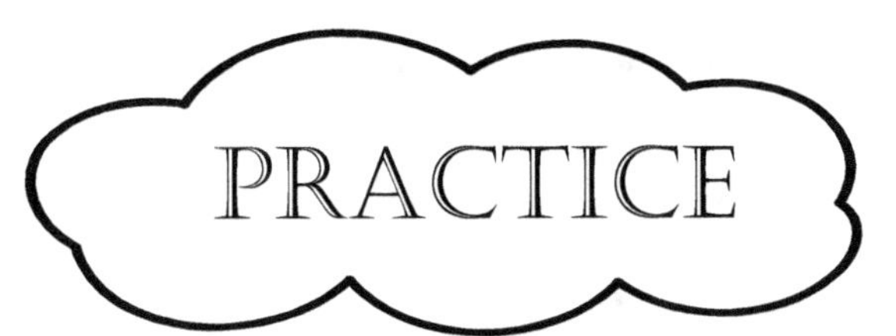
PRACTICE

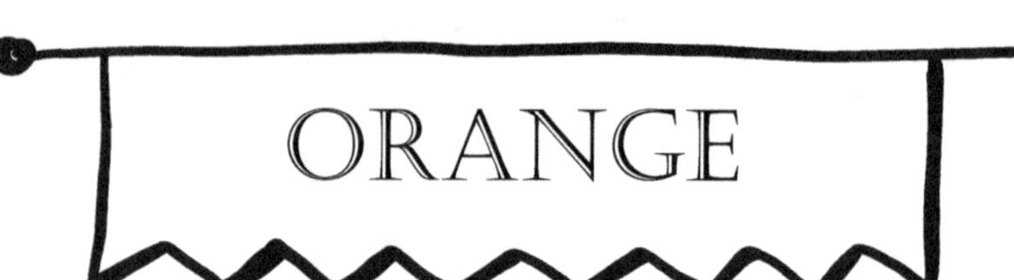

Step 1

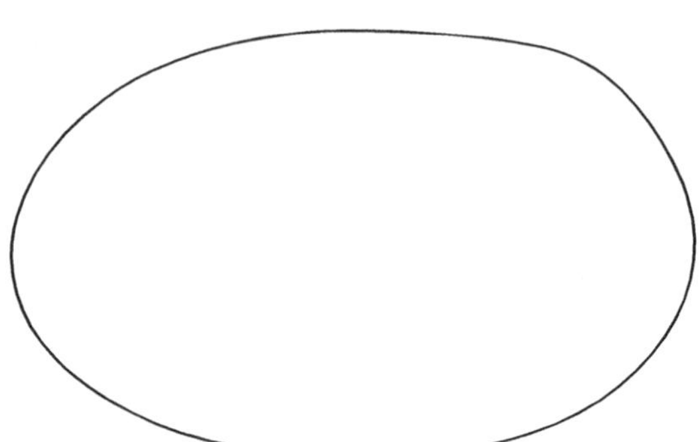

Step 2

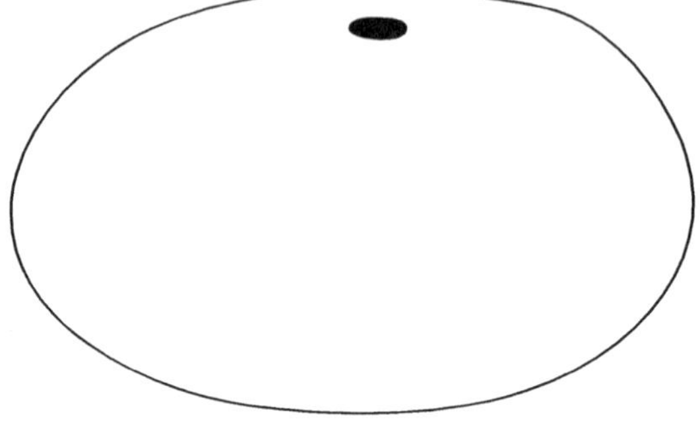

Step 3

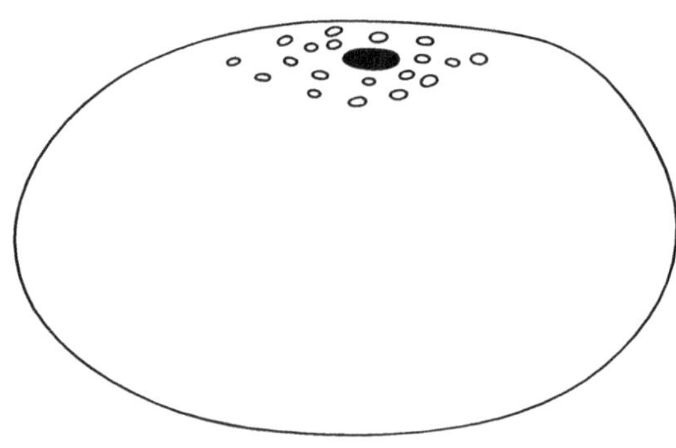

Step 4

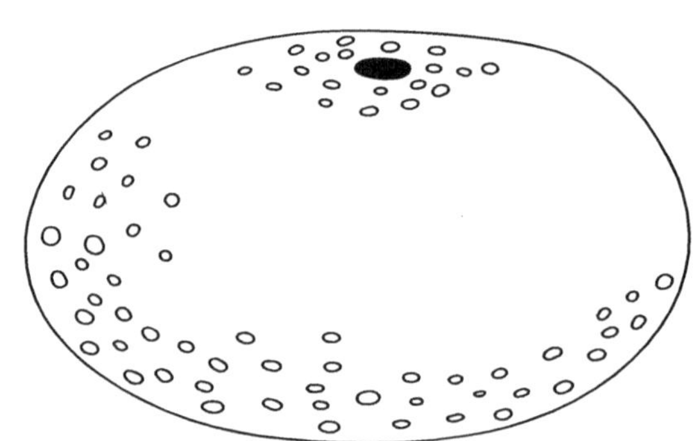

Step 5

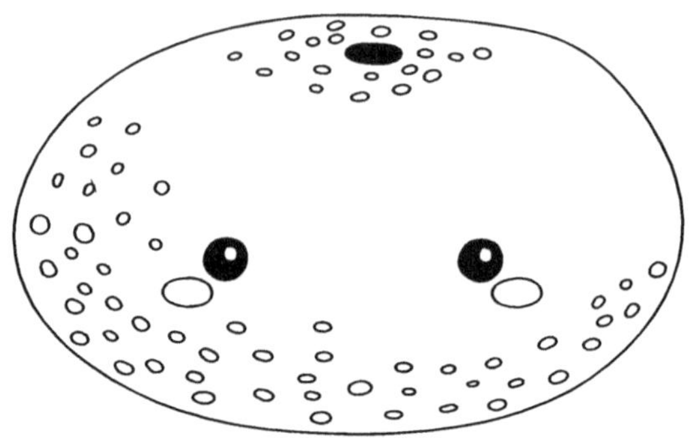

Step 6

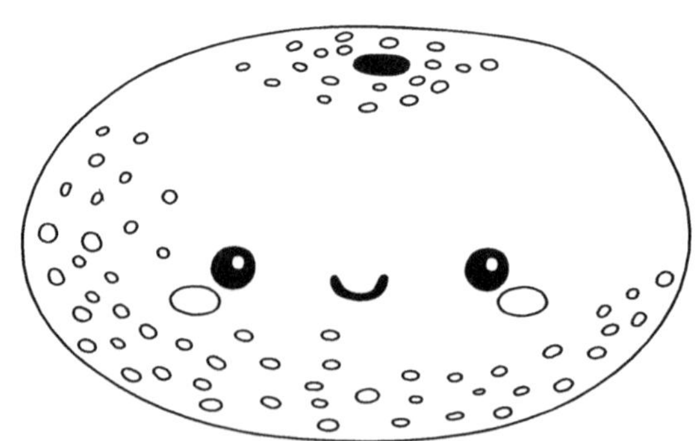

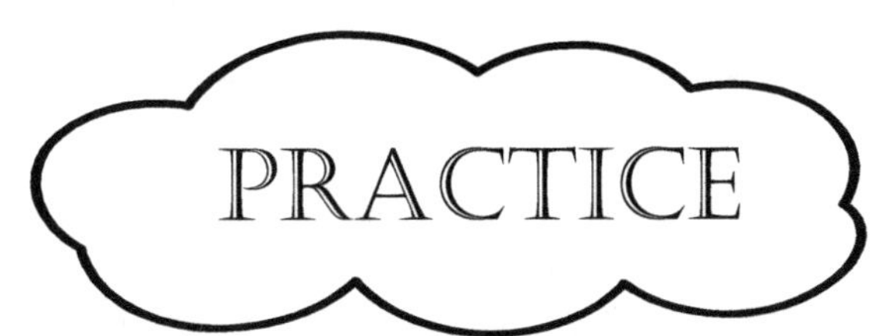
PRACTICE

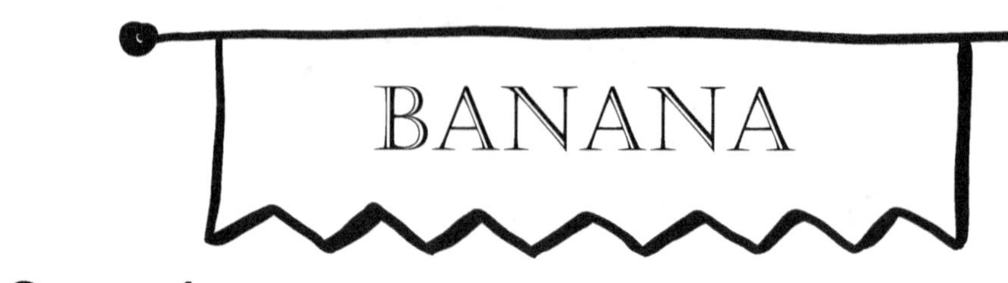

Step 1

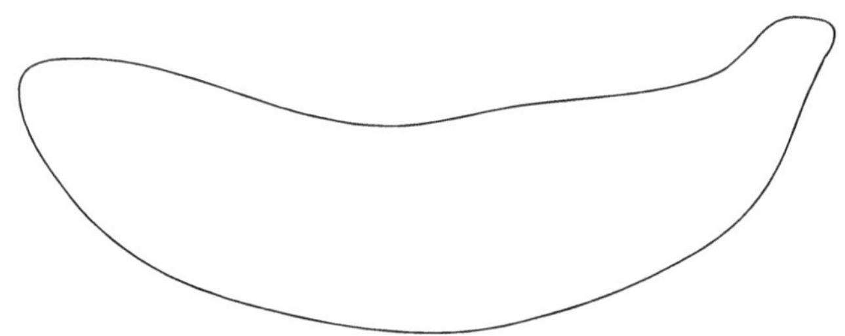

Step 2

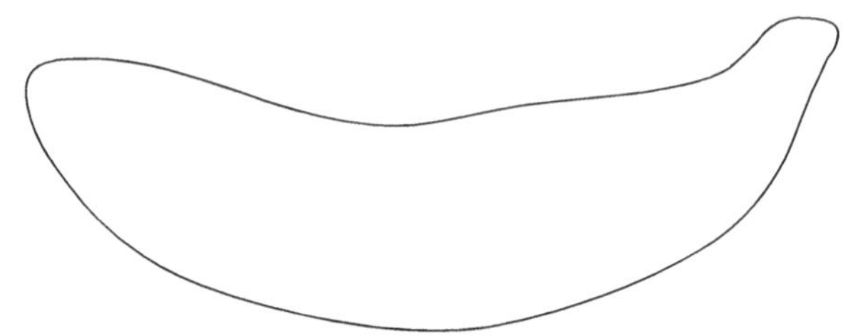

Step 3

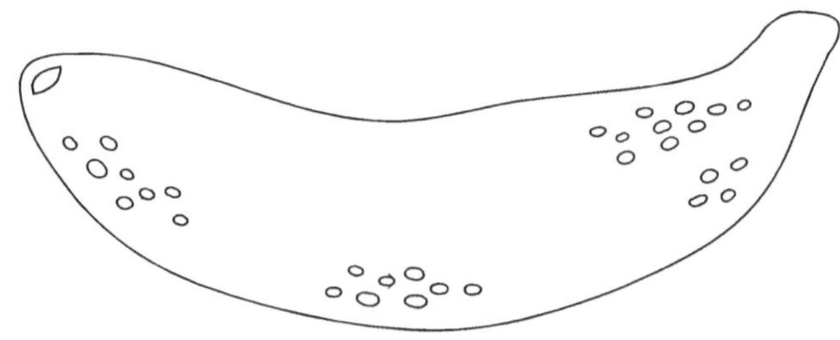

Step 4

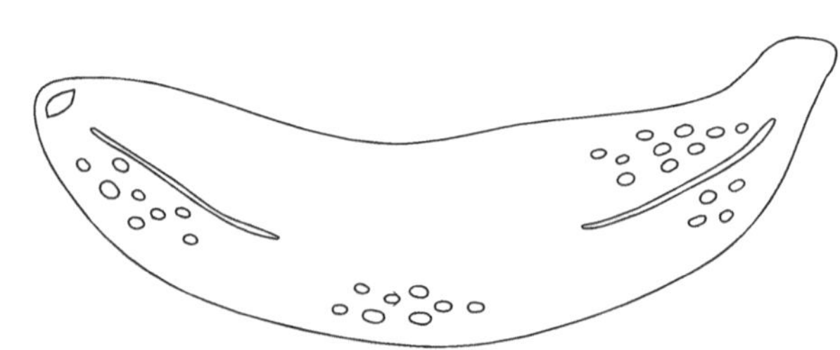

Step 5

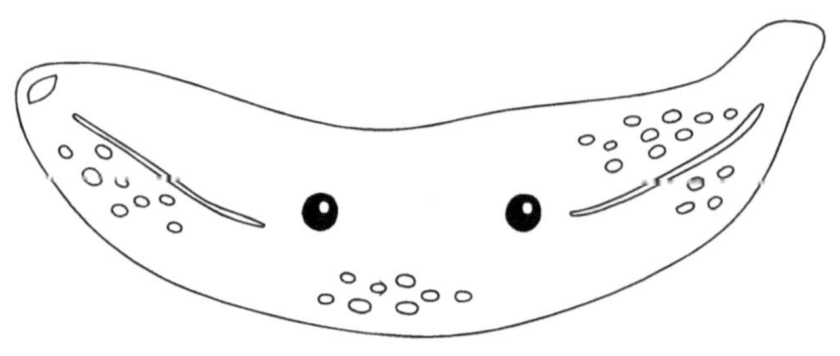

Step 6

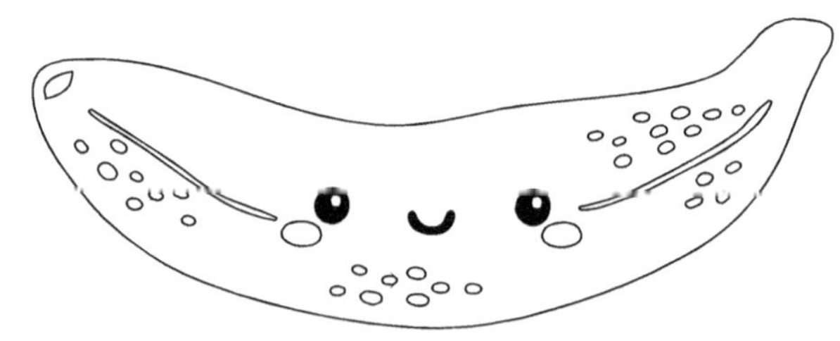

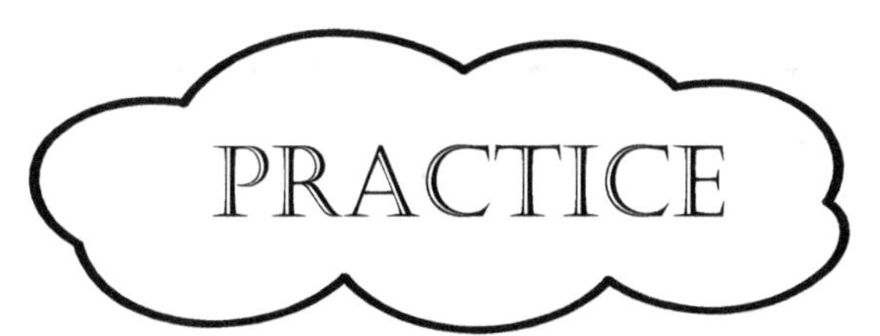
PRACTICE

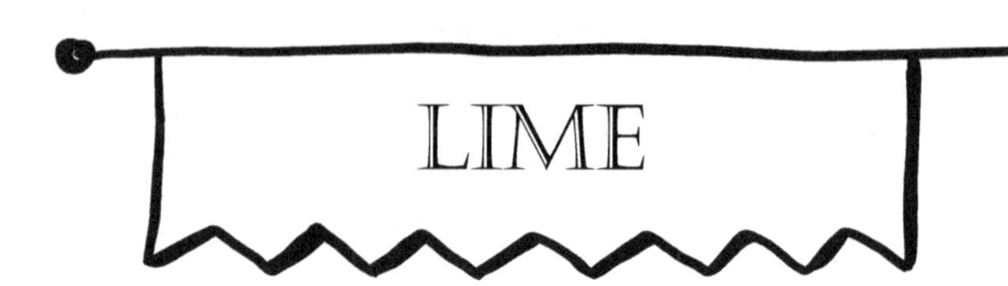

Step 1

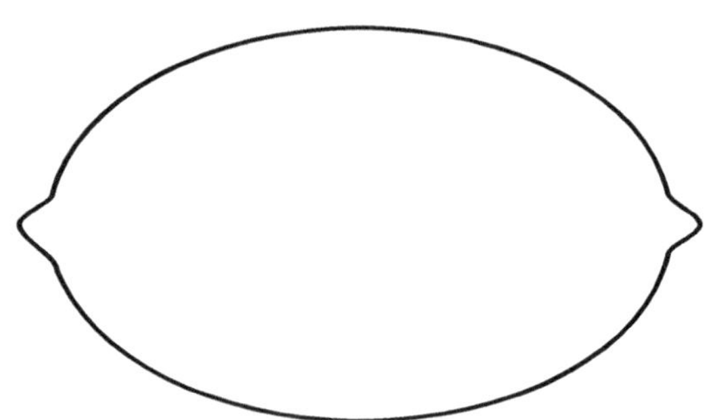

Step 2

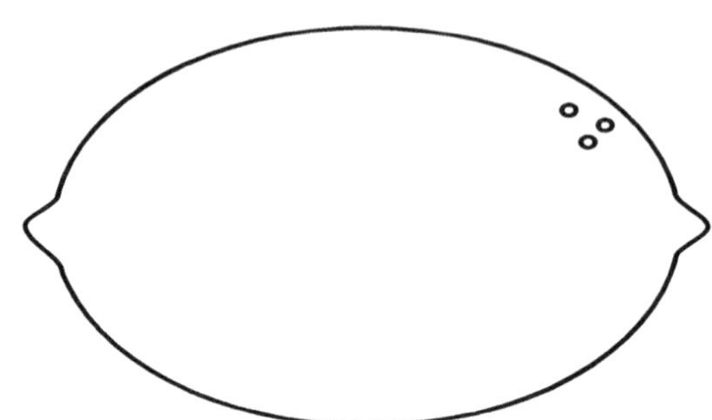

Step 3

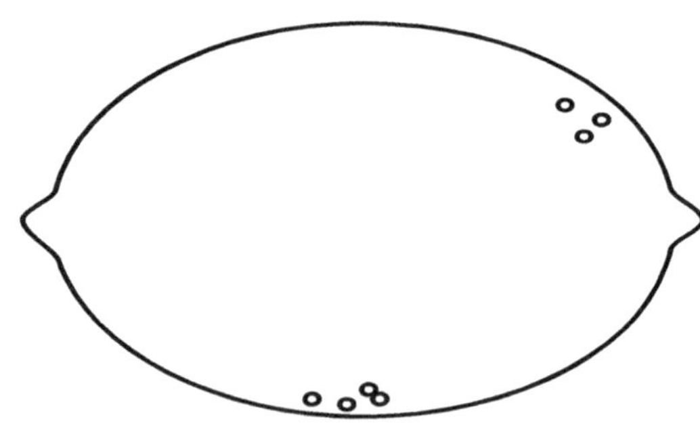

Step 4

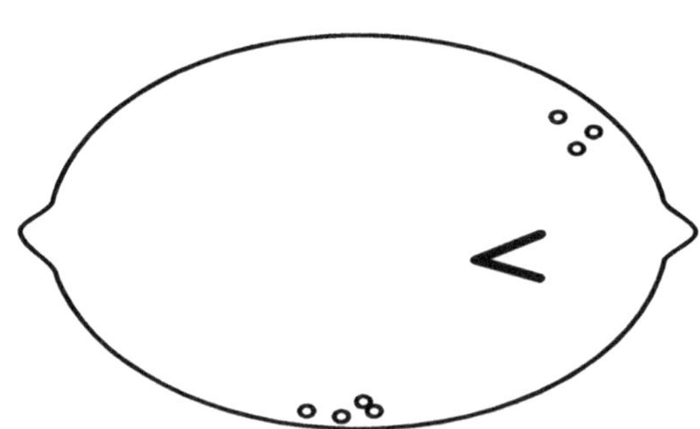

Step 5

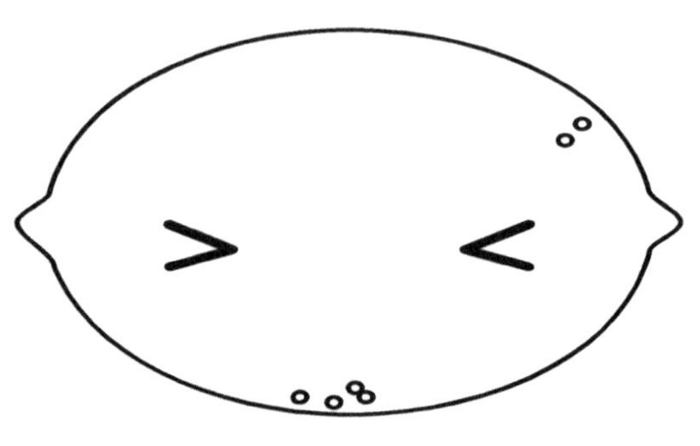

Step 6

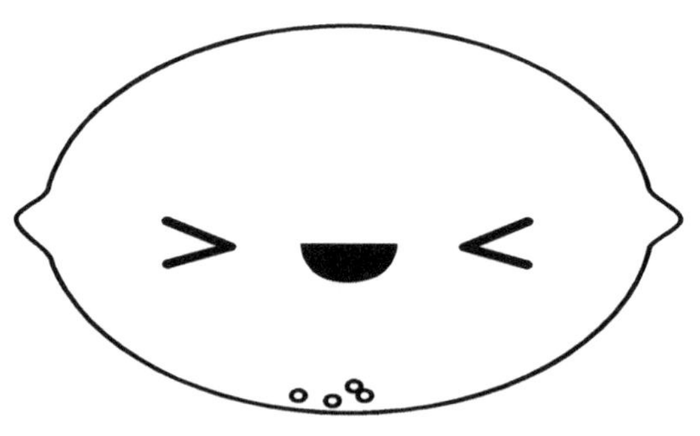

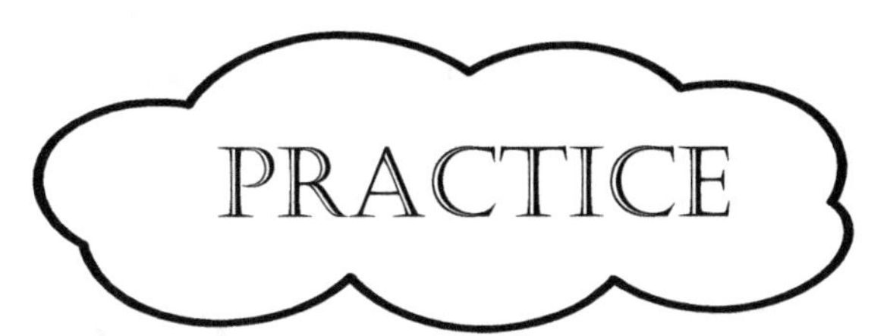
PRACTICE

BEAR

Step 1

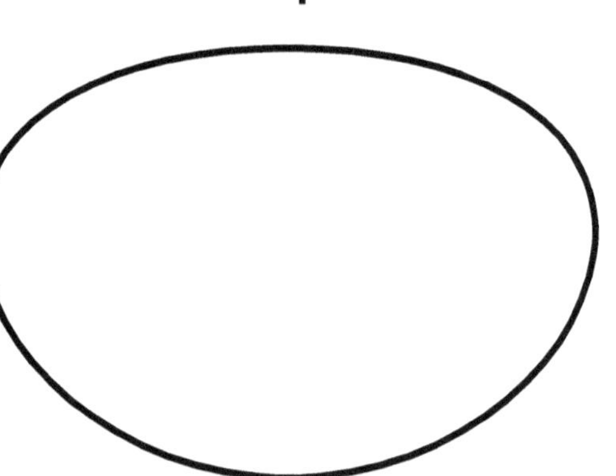

Step 2

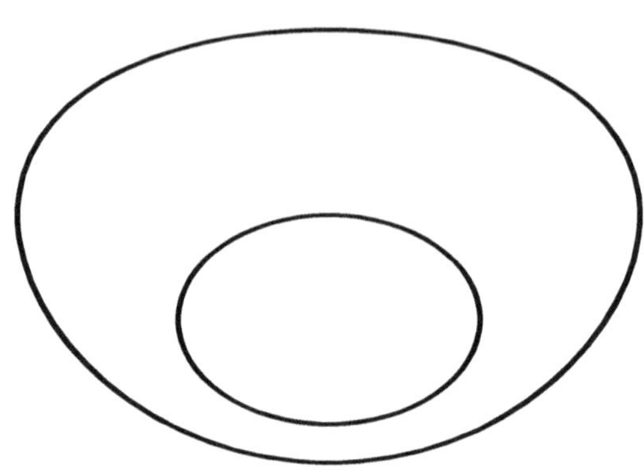

Step 3

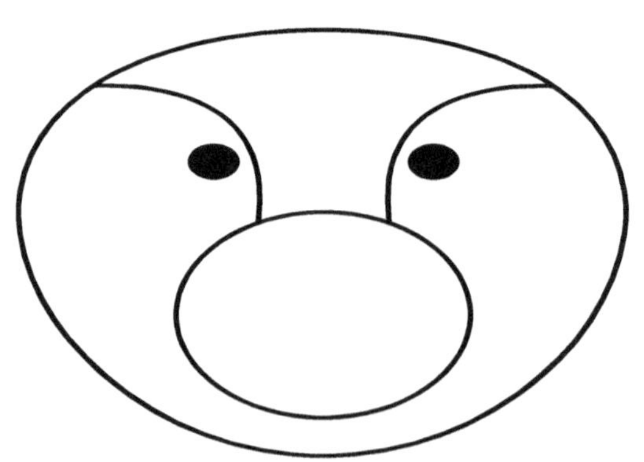

Step 4

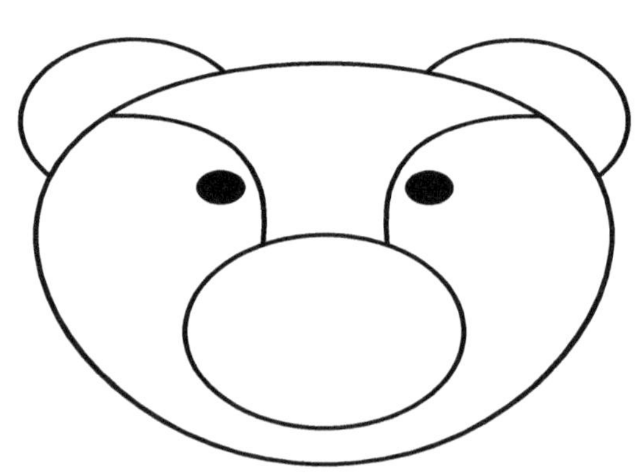

Step 5

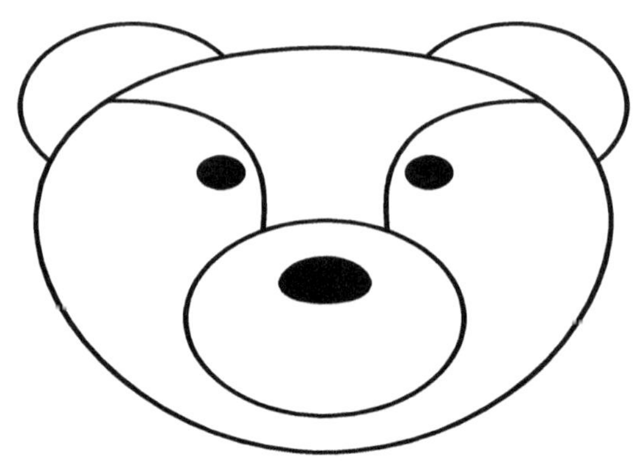

Step 6

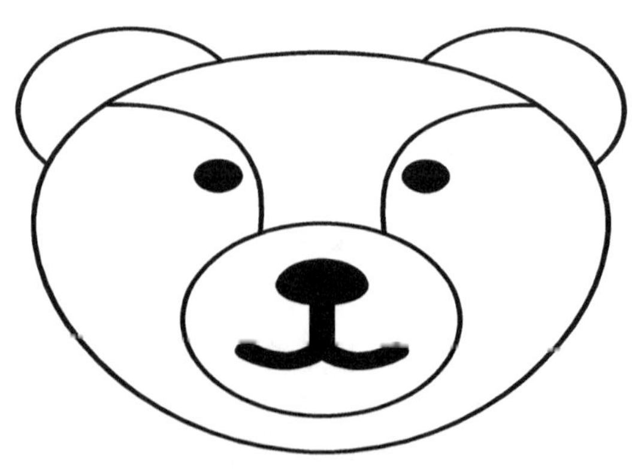

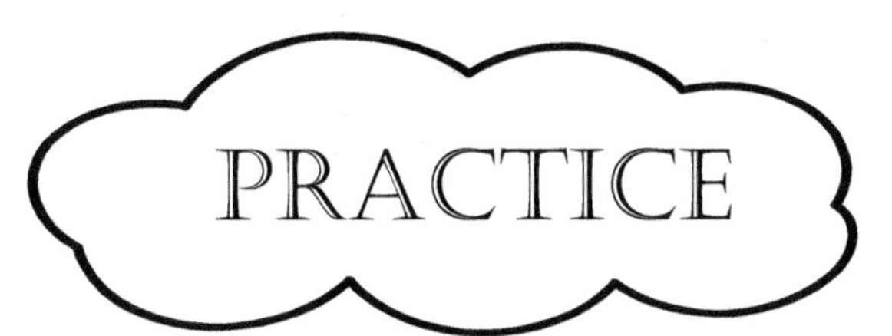
PRACTICE

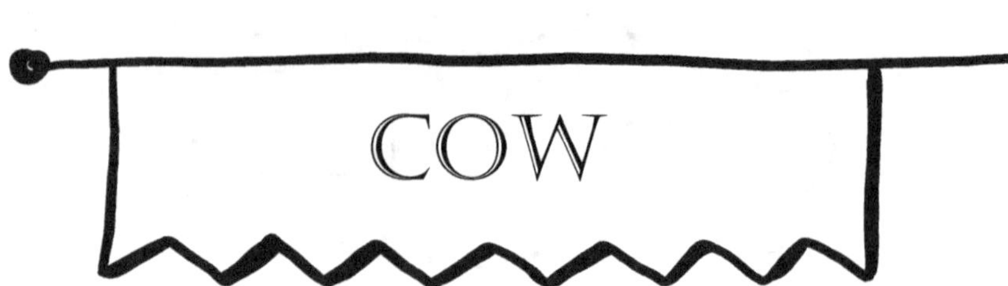

Step 1

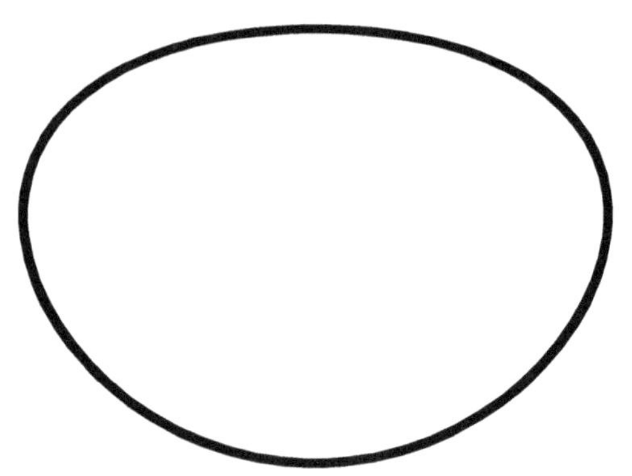

Step 2

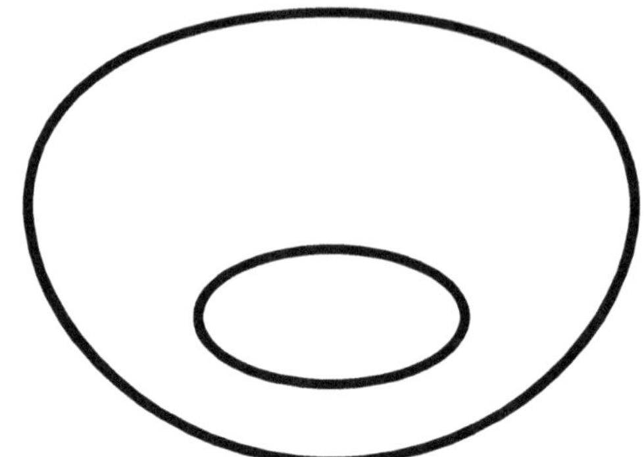

Step 3

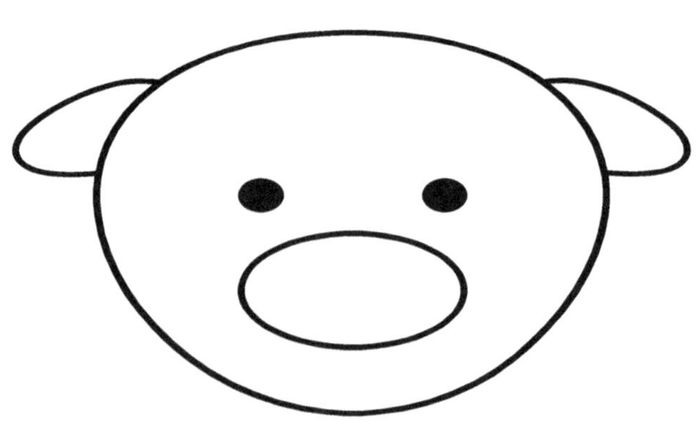

Step 4

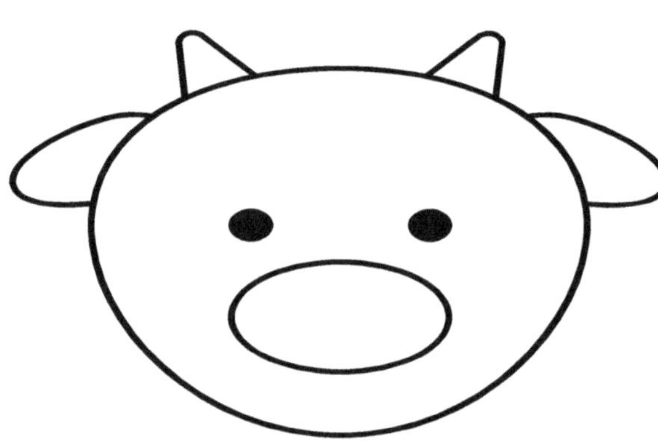

Step 5

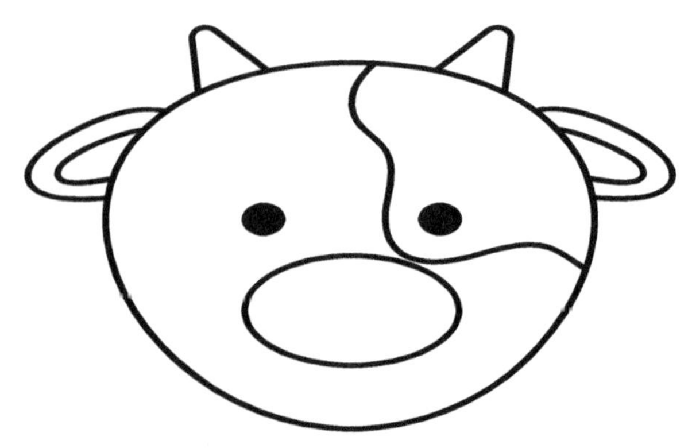

Step 6

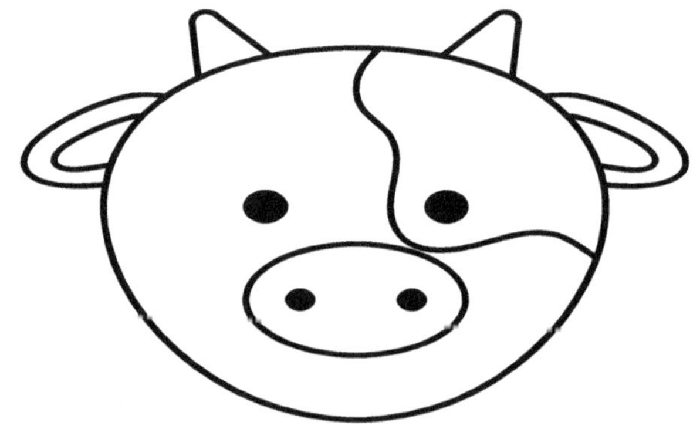

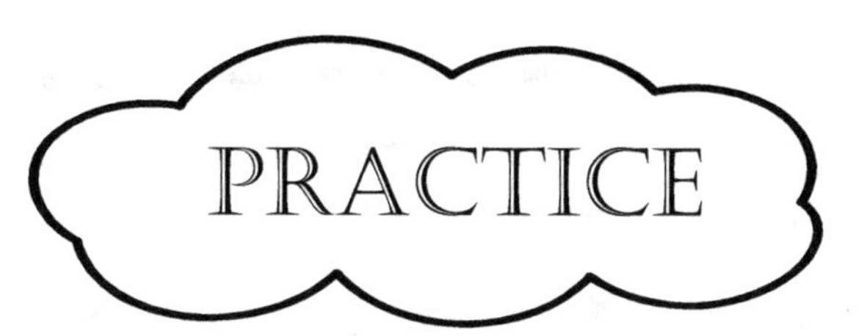
PRACTICE

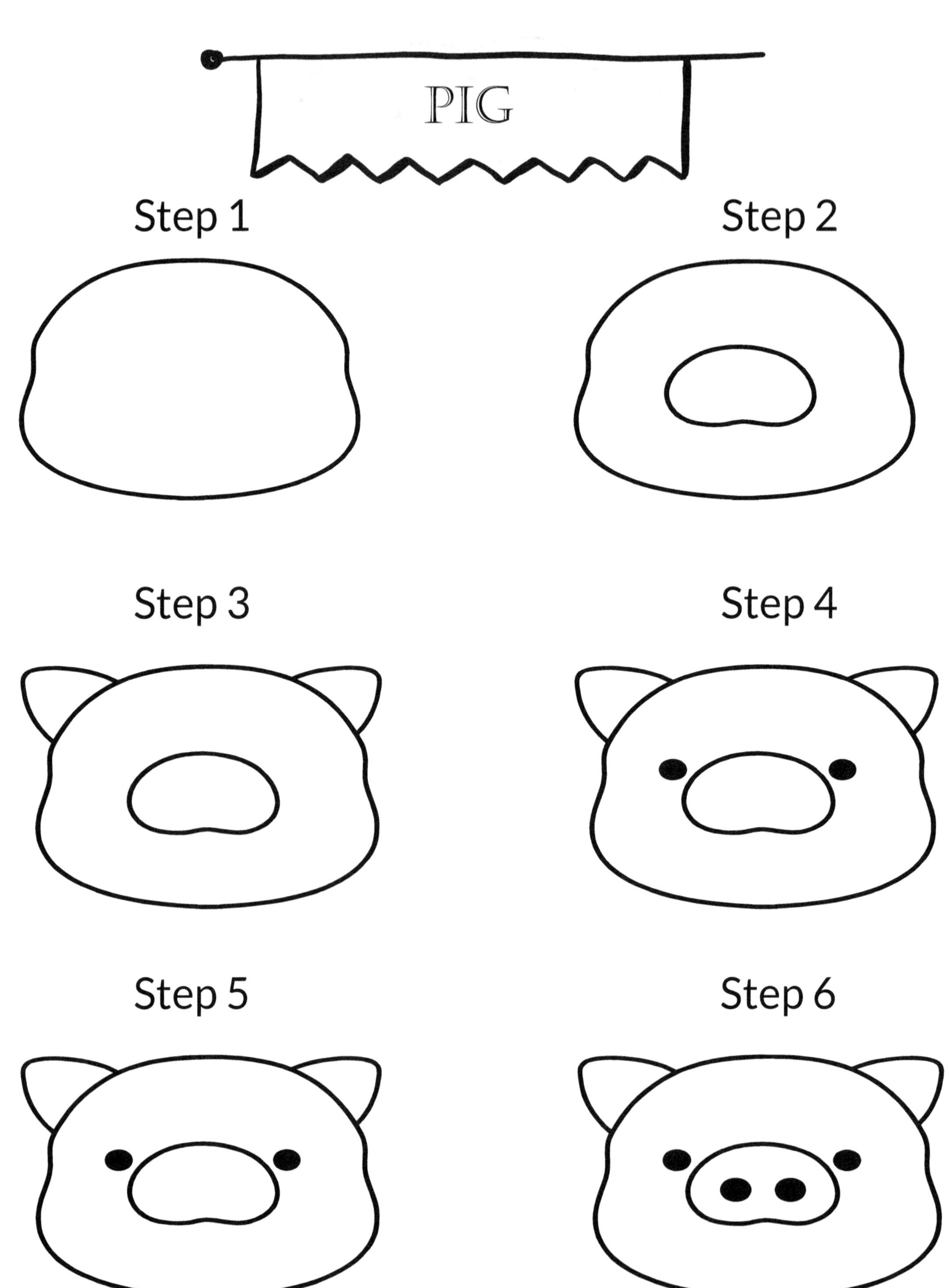
PIG
Step 1
Step 2
Step 3
Step 4
Step 5
Step 6

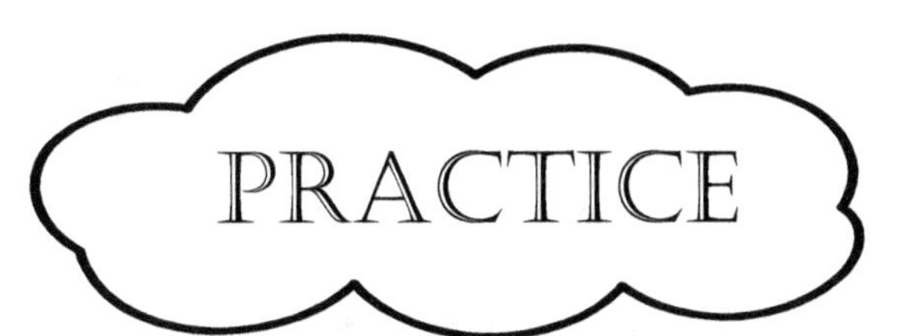
PRACTICE

BADGER

Step 1

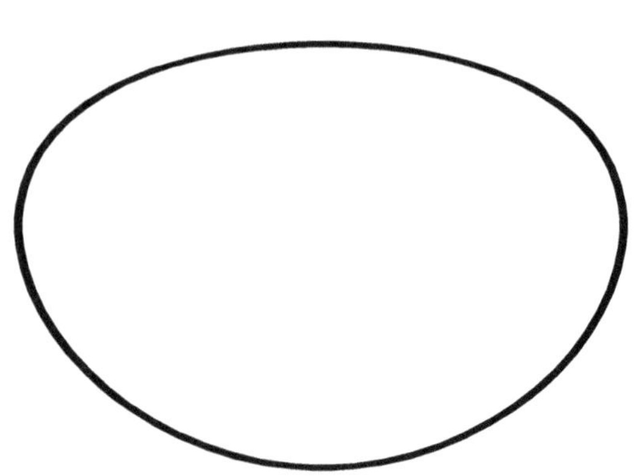

Step 2

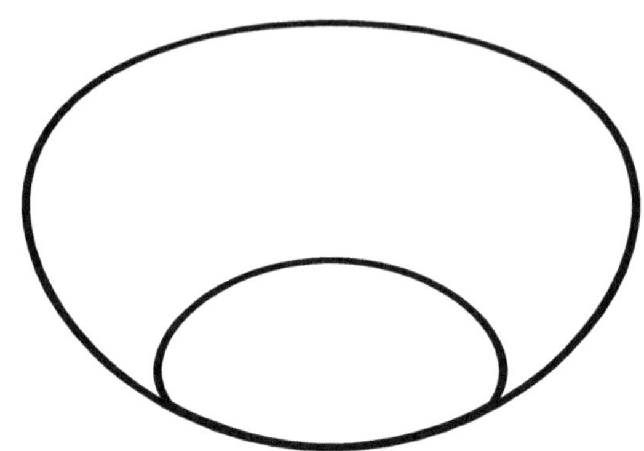

Step 3

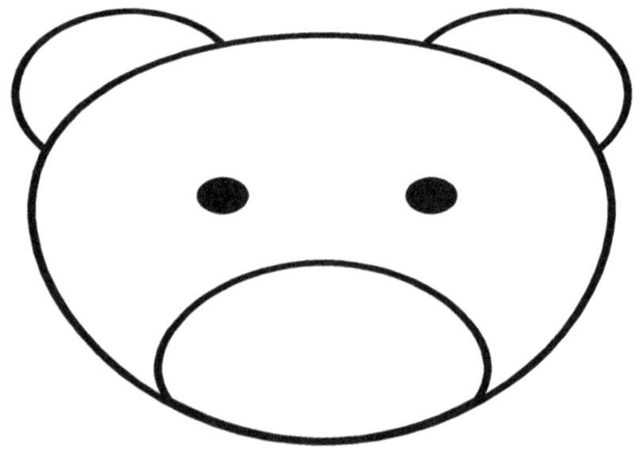

Step 4

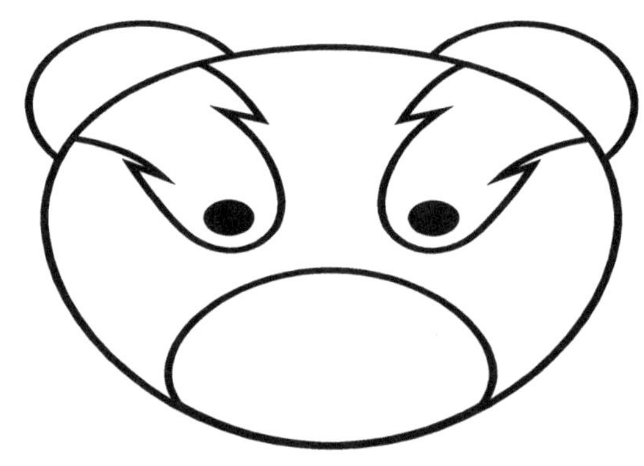

Step 5

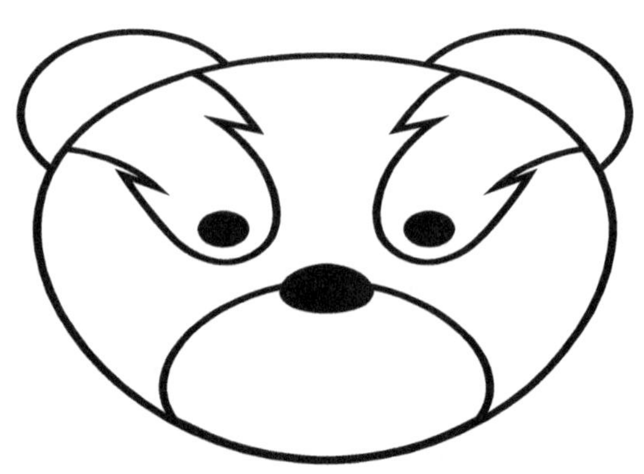

Step 6

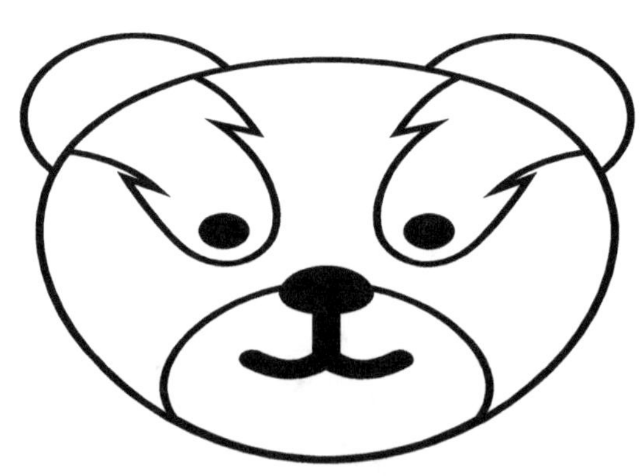

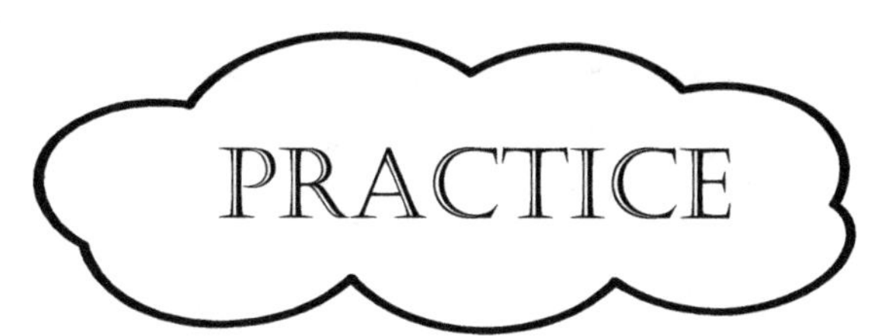
PRACTICE

PLATYPUS

Step 1

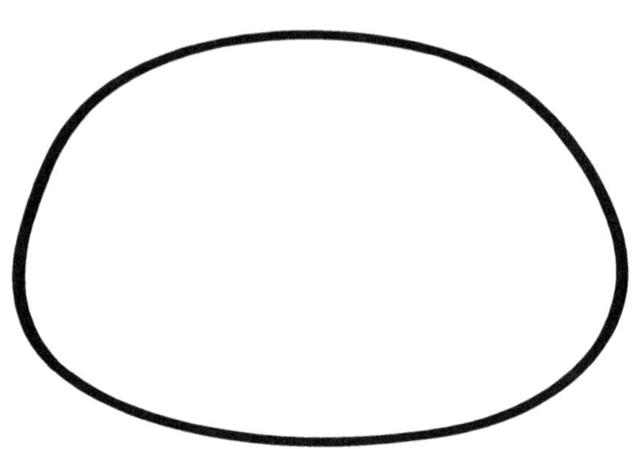

Step 2

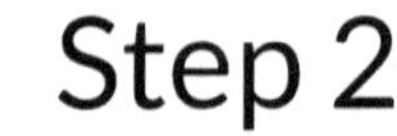

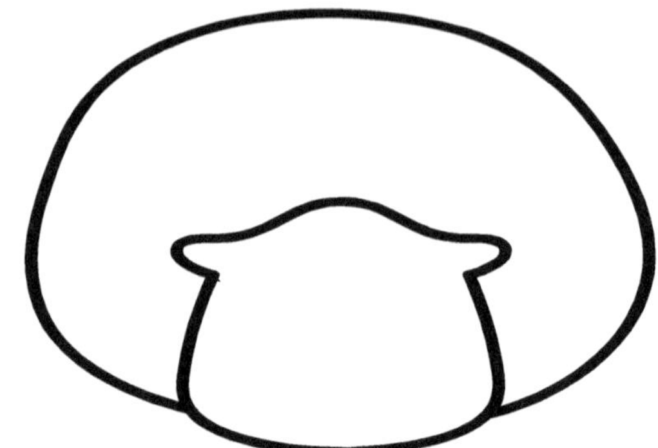

Step 3

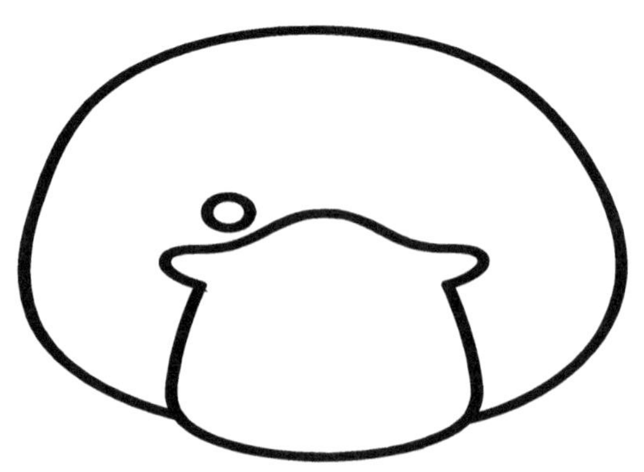

Step 4

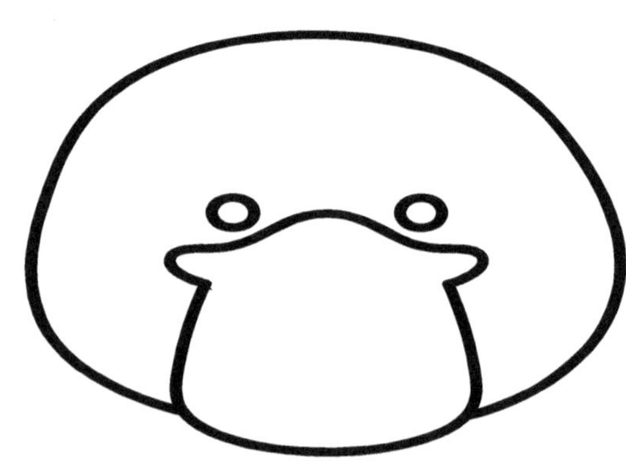

Step 5

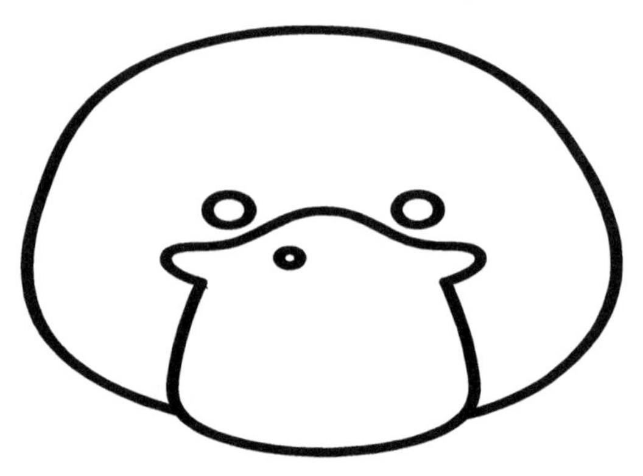

Step 6

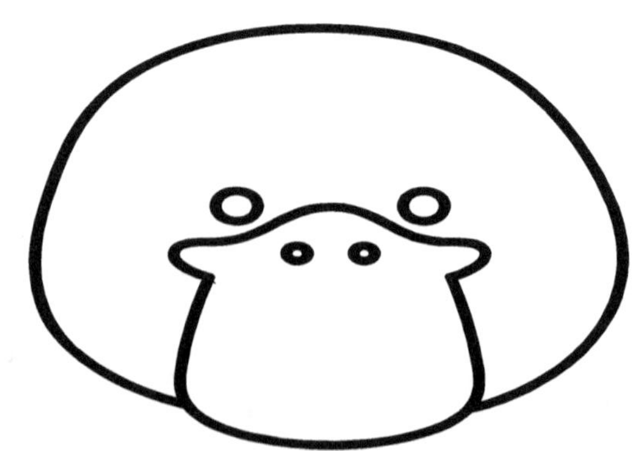

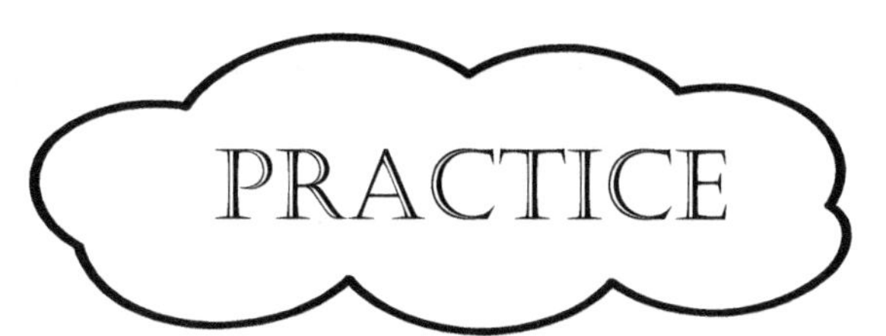
PRACTICE

DEER

Step 1

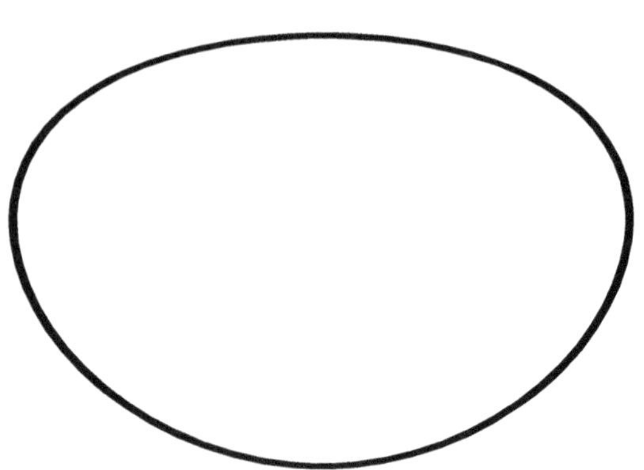

Step 2

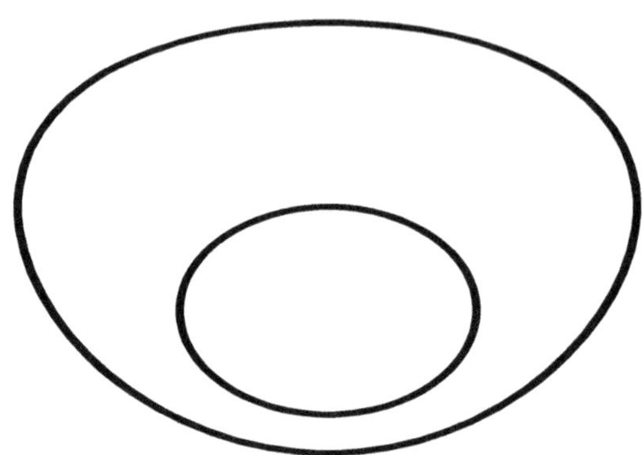

Step 3

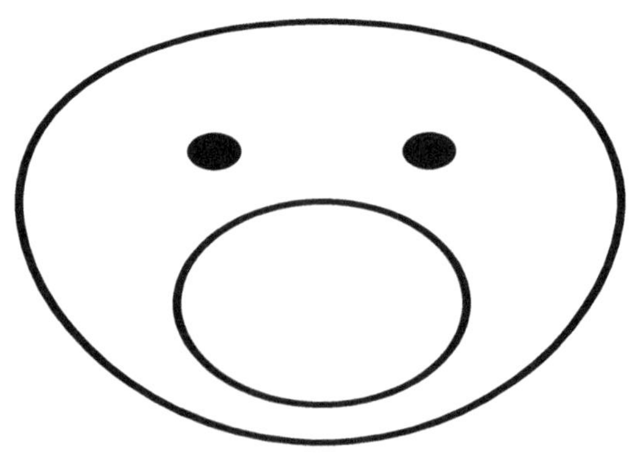

Step 4

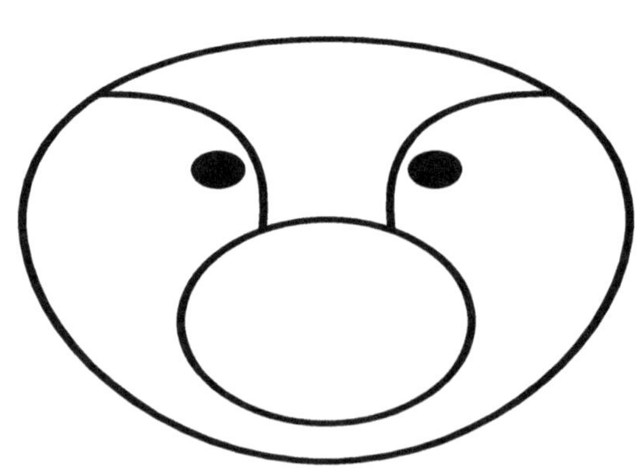

Step 5

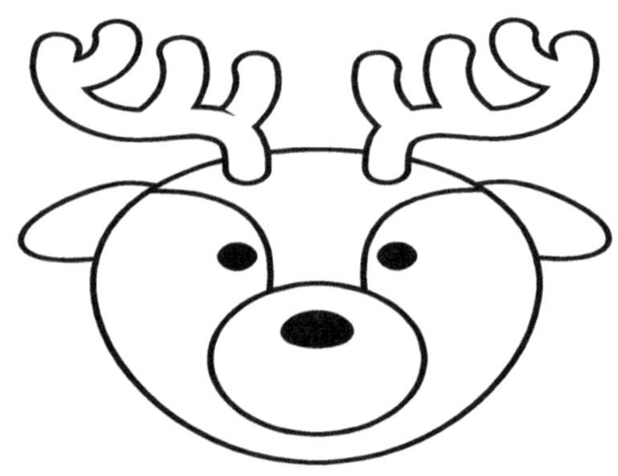

Step 6

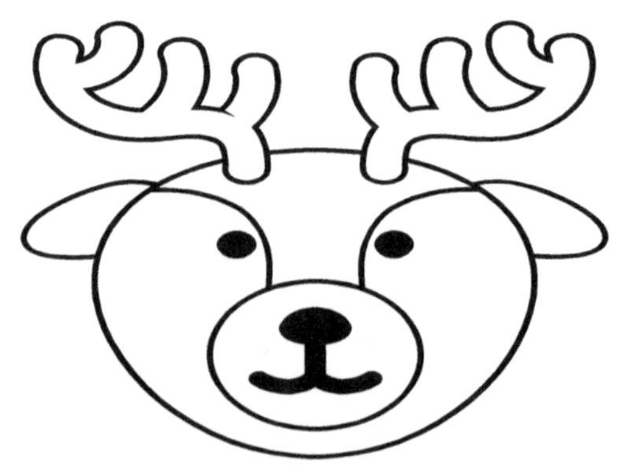

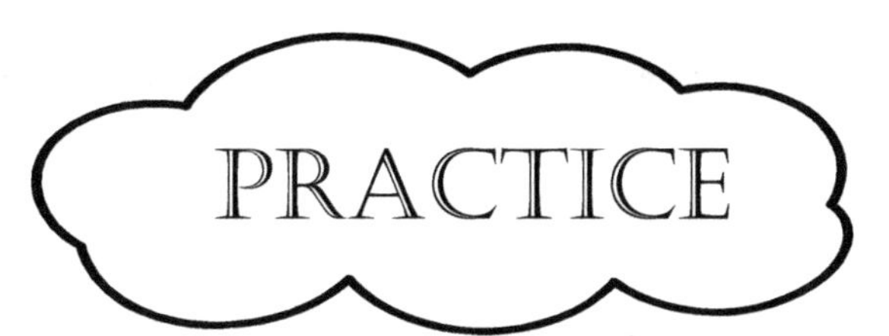
PRACTICE

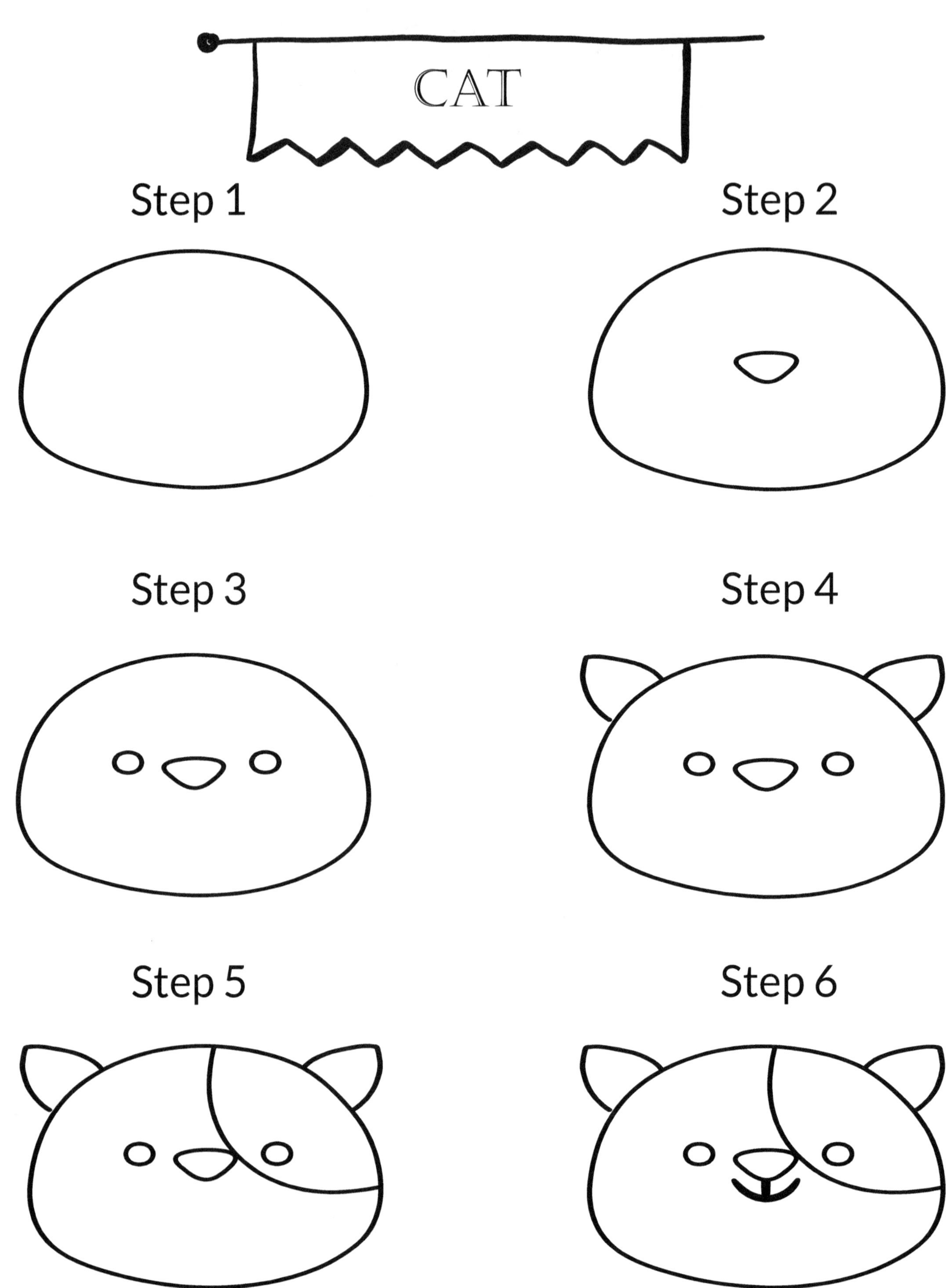
CAT
Step 1
Step 2
Step 3
Step 4
Step 5
Step 6

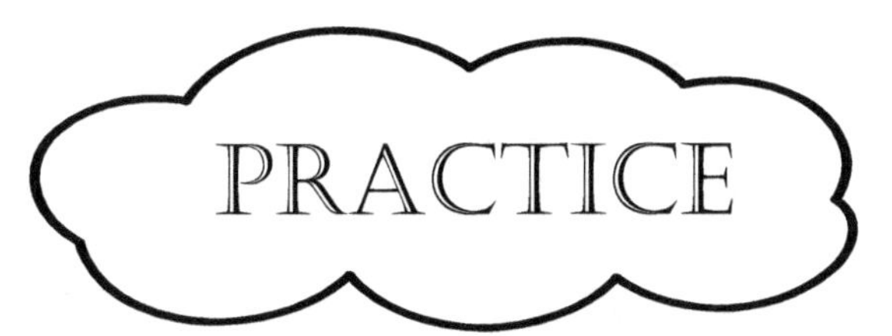
PRACTICE

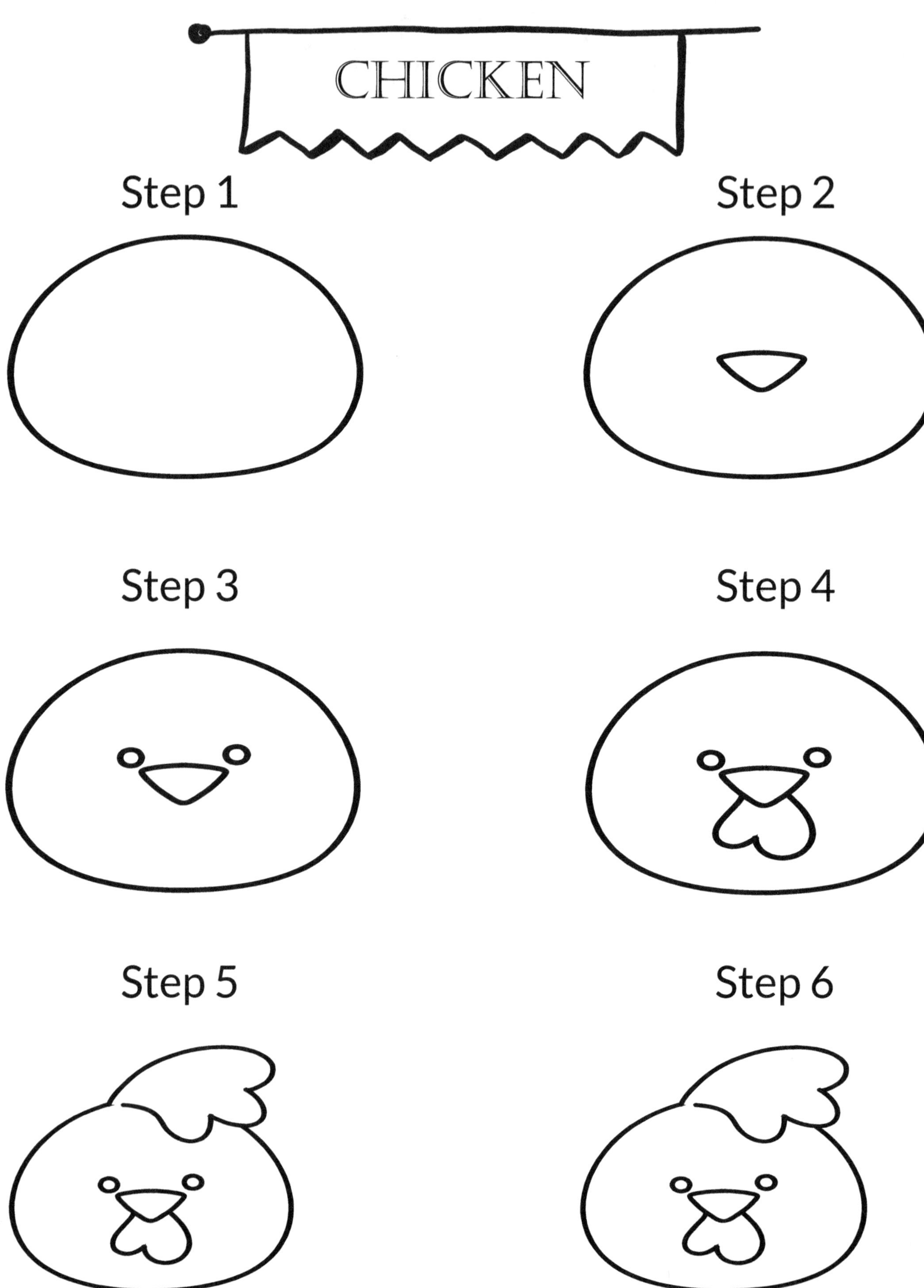
CHICKEN
Step 1
Step 2
Step 3
Step 4
Step 5
Step 6

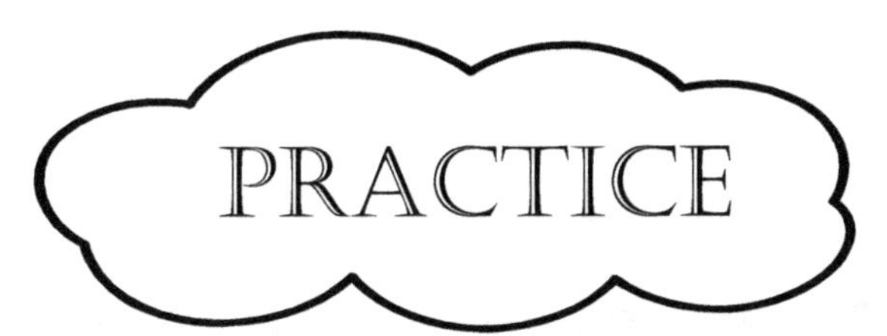
PRACTICE

GOAT

Step 1

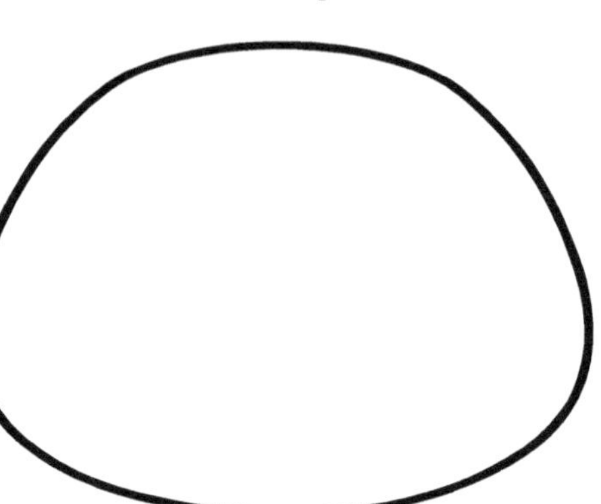

Step 2

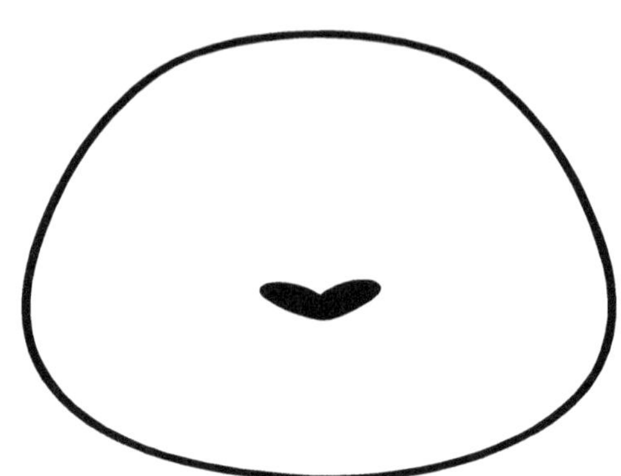

Step 3

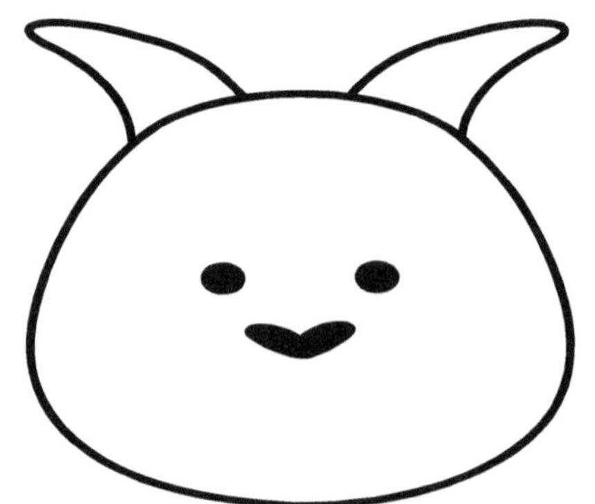

Step 4

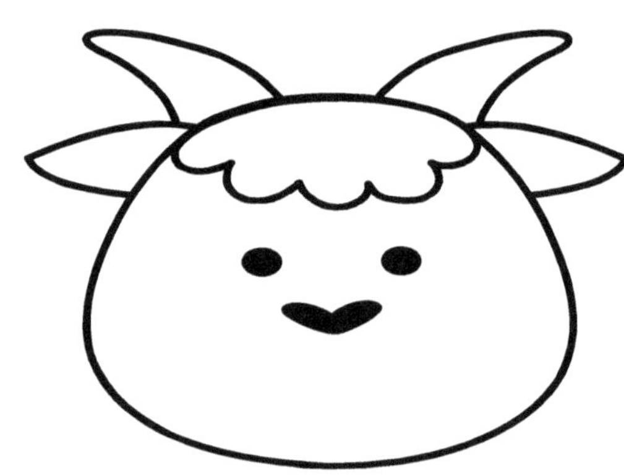

Step 5

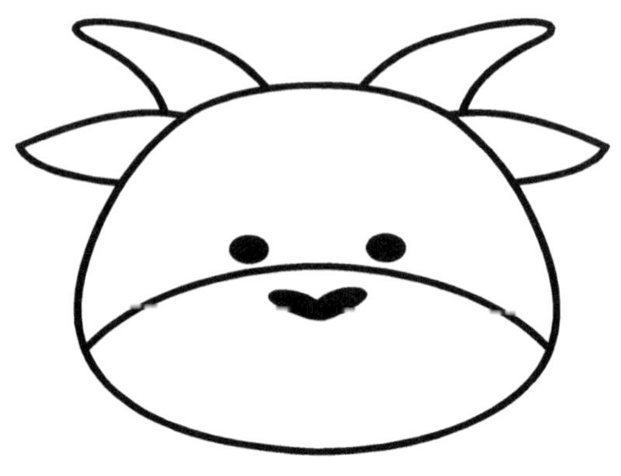

Step 6

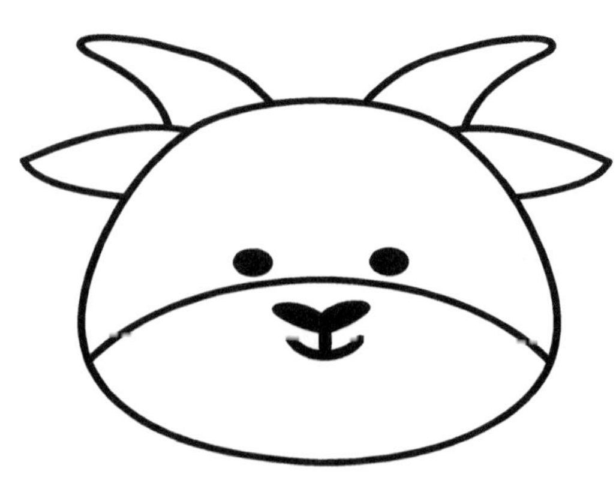

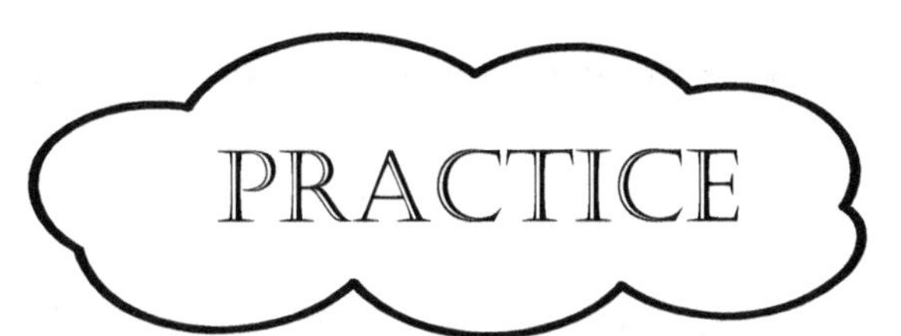
PRACTICE

BULL

Step 1

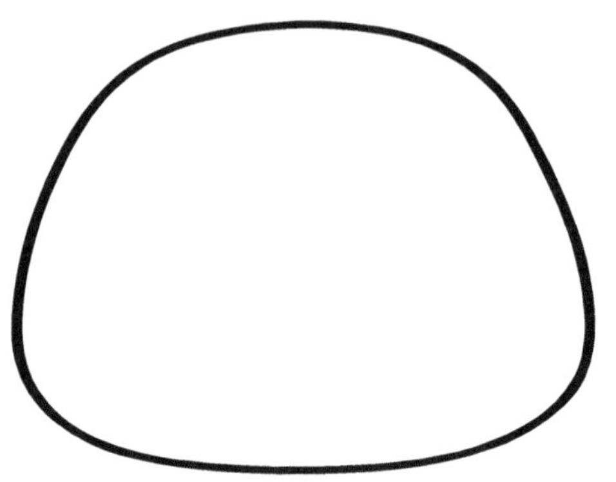

Step 2

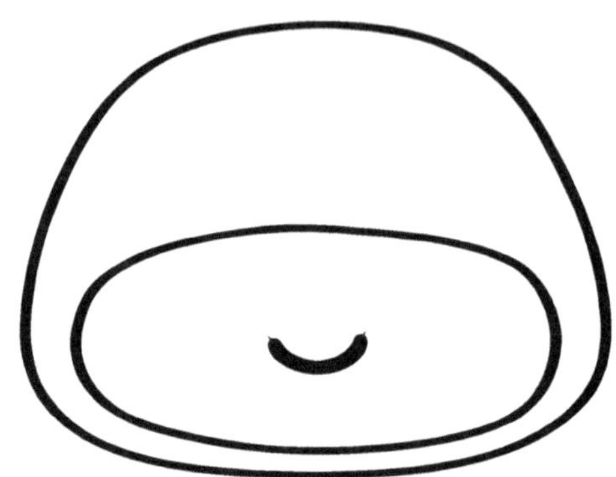

Step 3

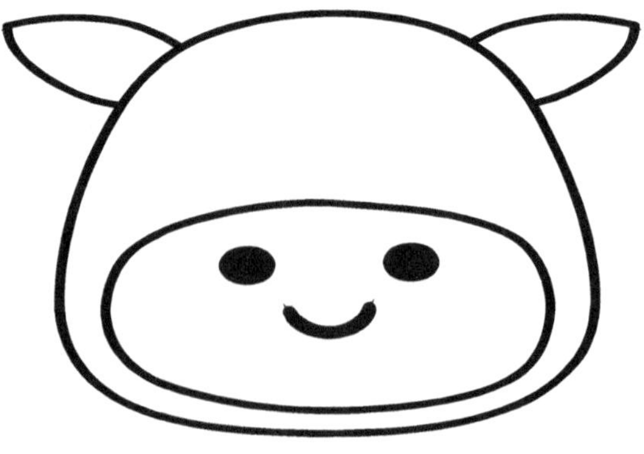

Step 4

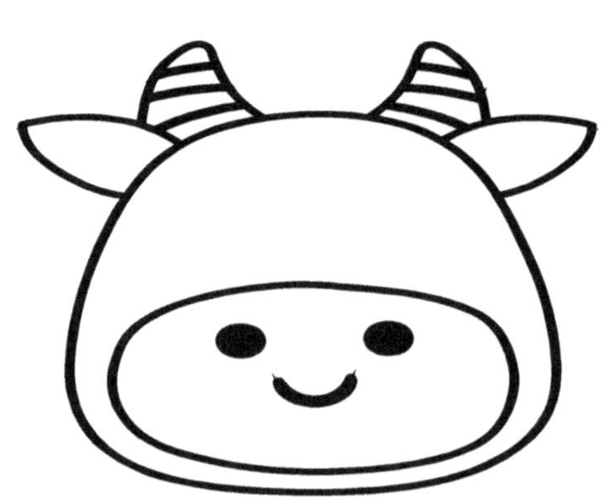

Step 5

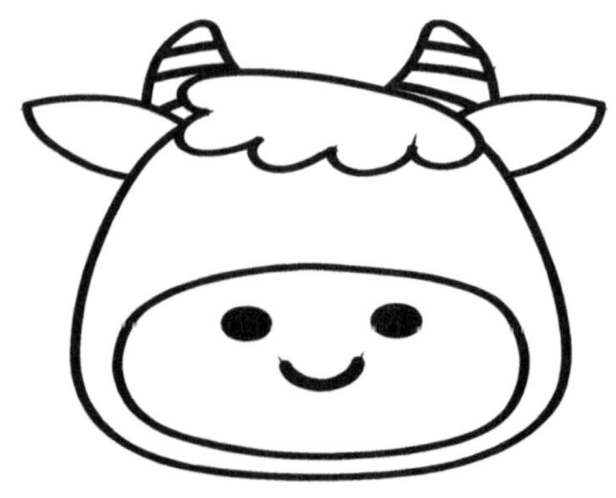

Step 6

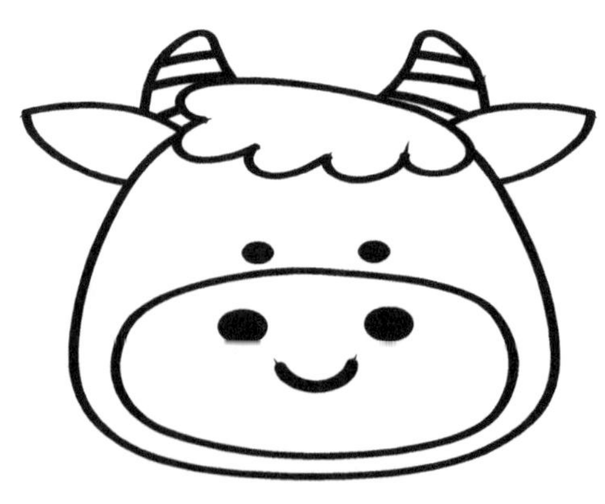

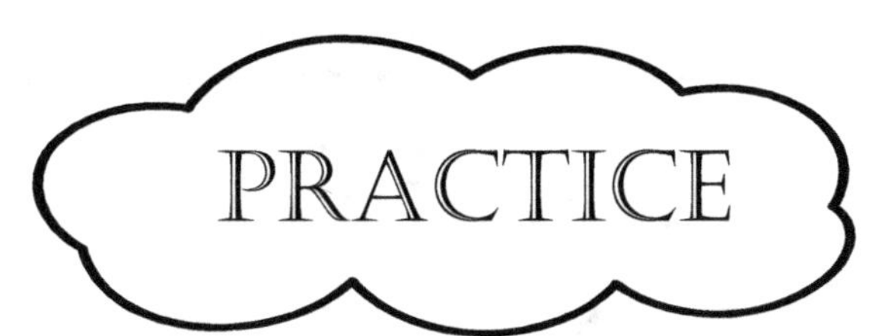
PRACTICE

RABBIT

Step 1

Step 2

Step 3

Step 4

Step 5

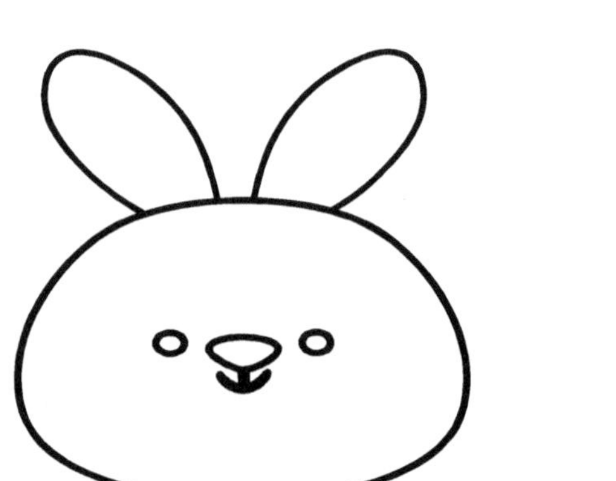

Step 6

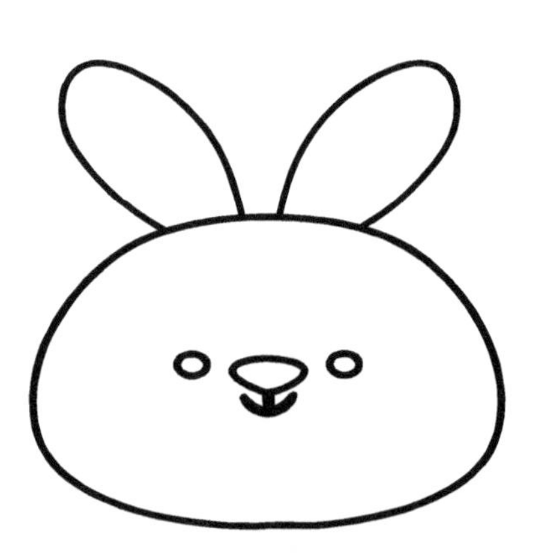

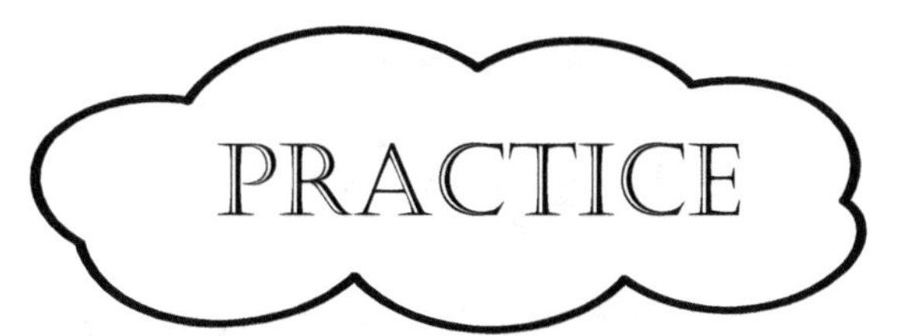
PRACTICE

HORSE

Step 1

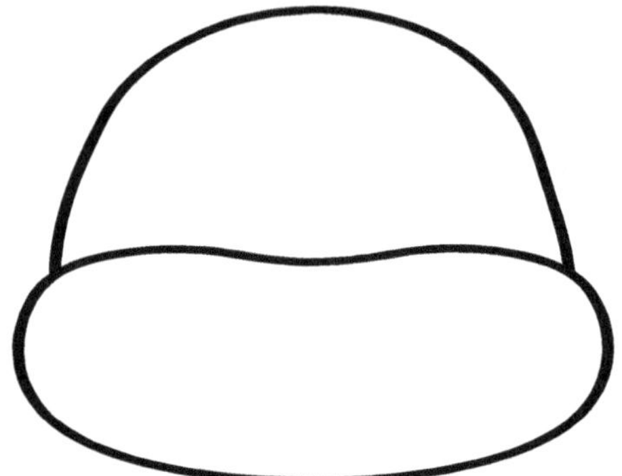

Step 2

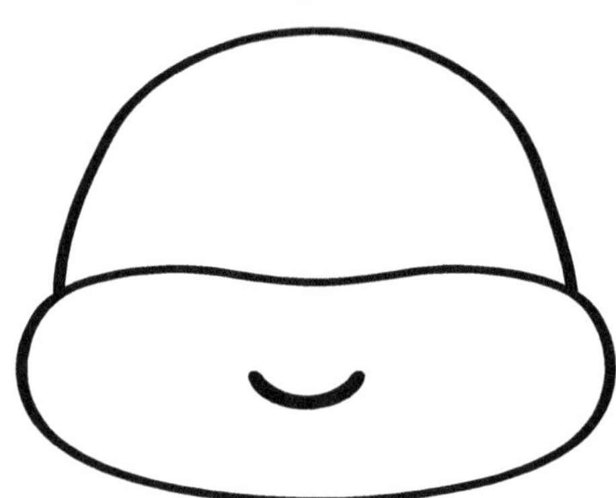

Step 3

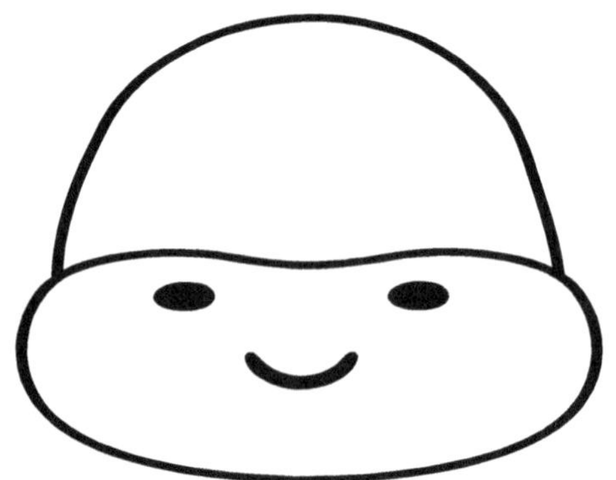

Step 4

Step 5

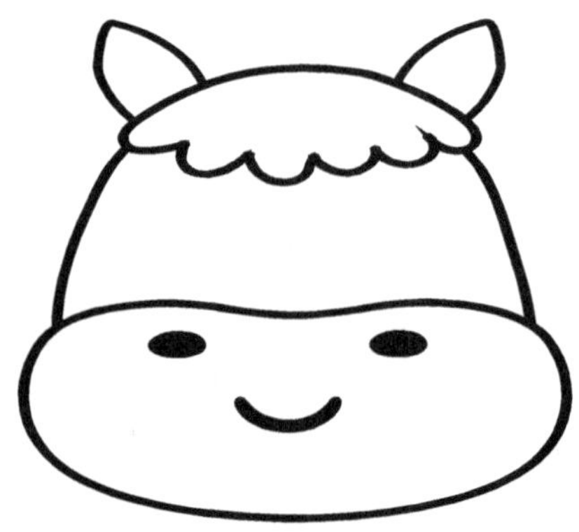

Step 6

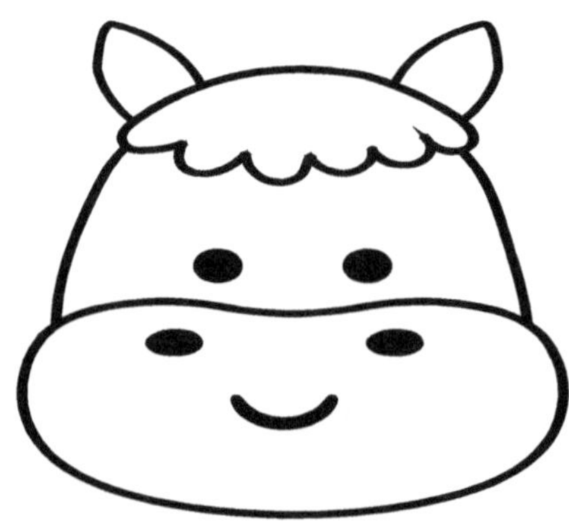

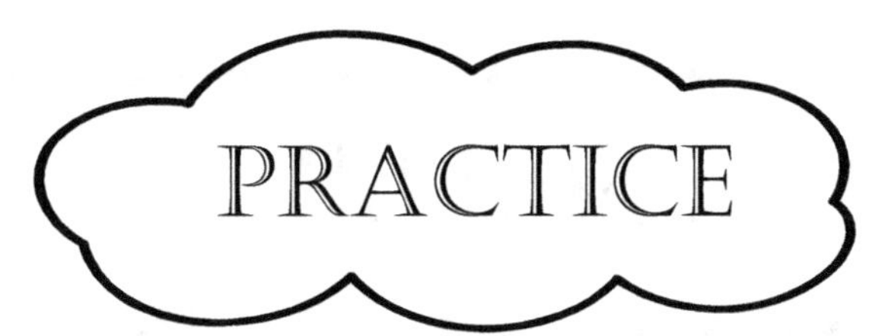
PRACTICE

SHEEP

Step 1

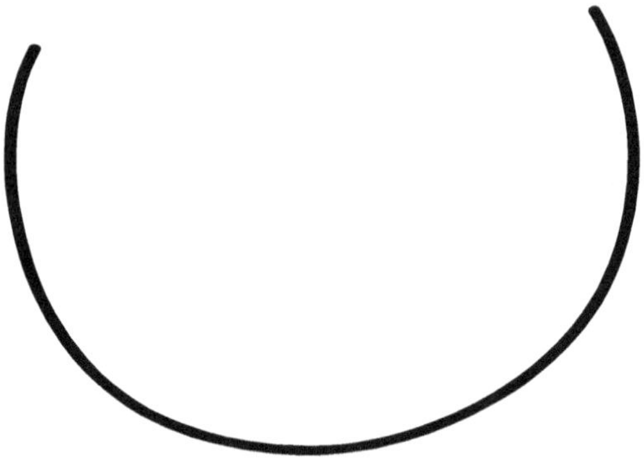

Step 2

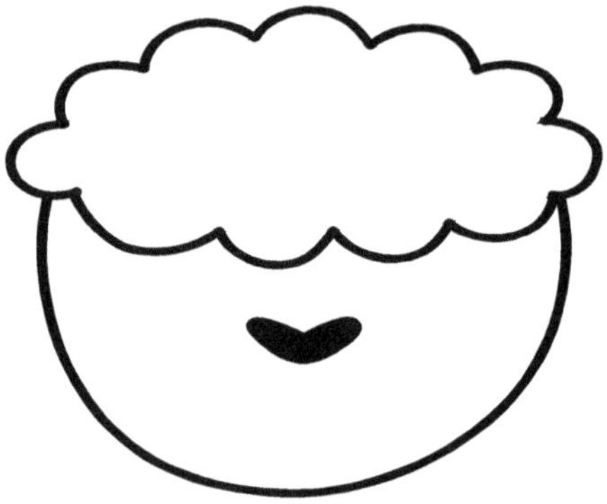

Step 3

Step 4

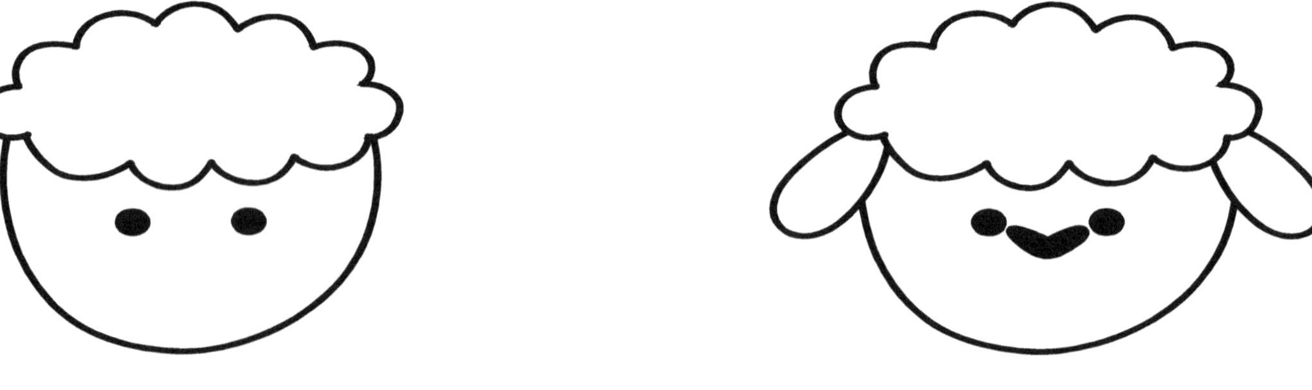

Step 5

Step 6

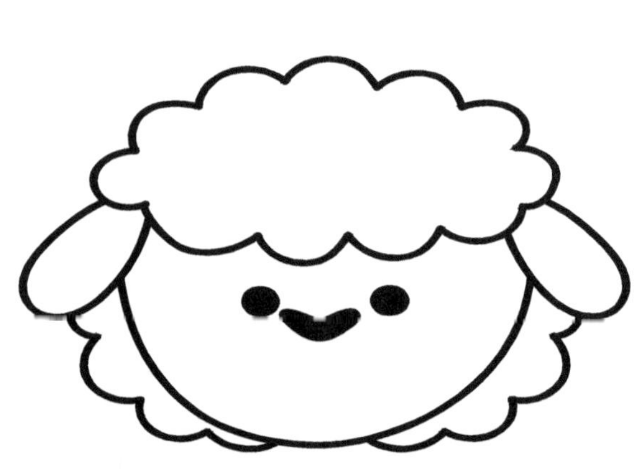

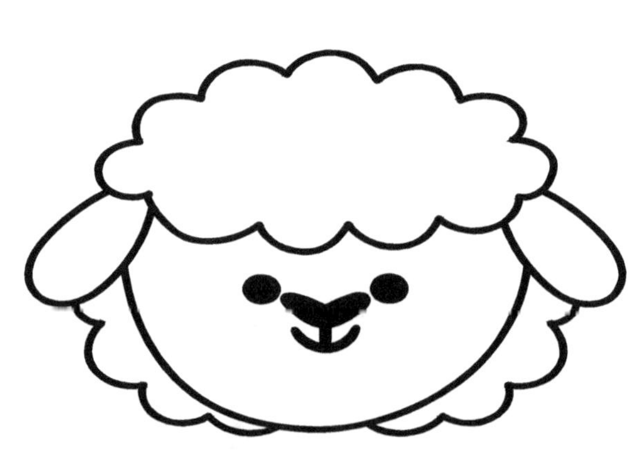

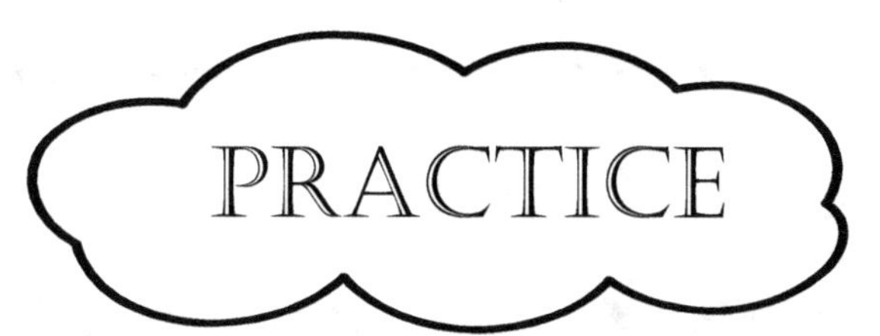
PRACTICE

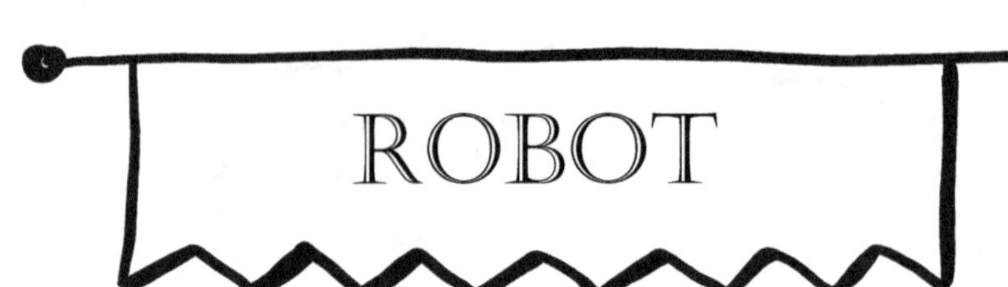

Step 1

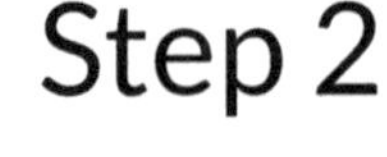

Step 2

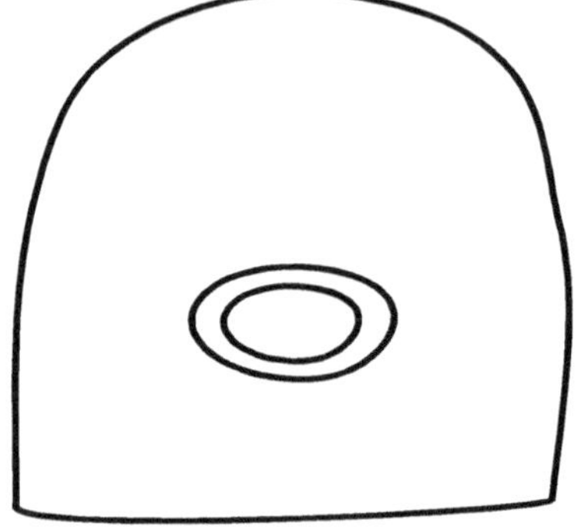

Step 3

Step 4

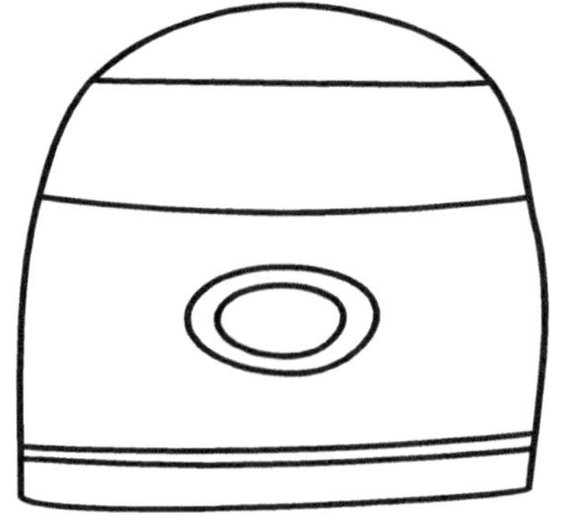

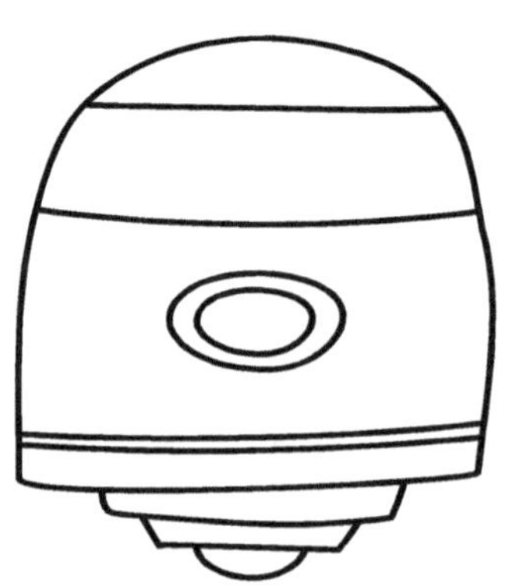

Step 5

Step 6

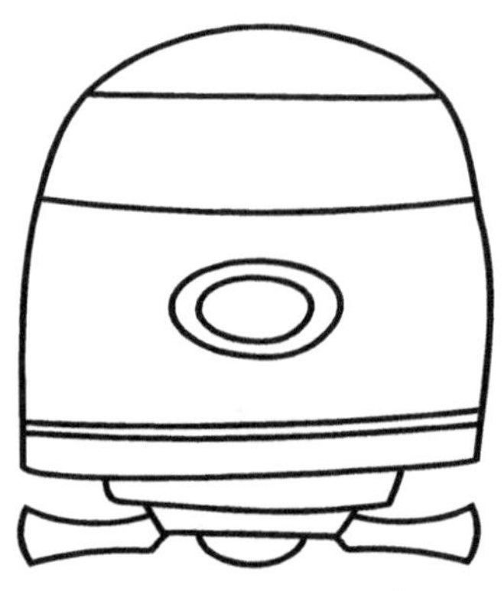

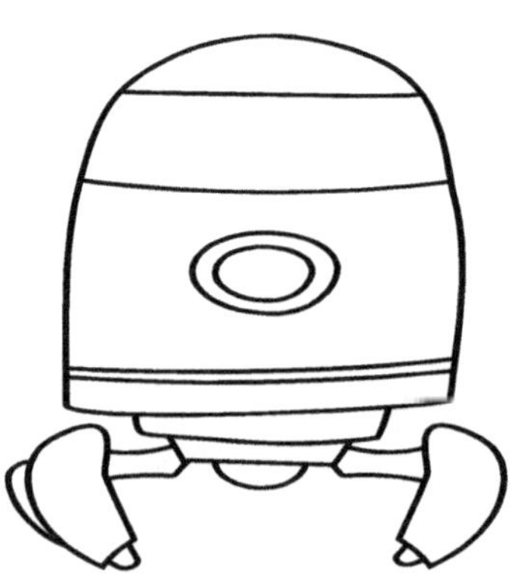

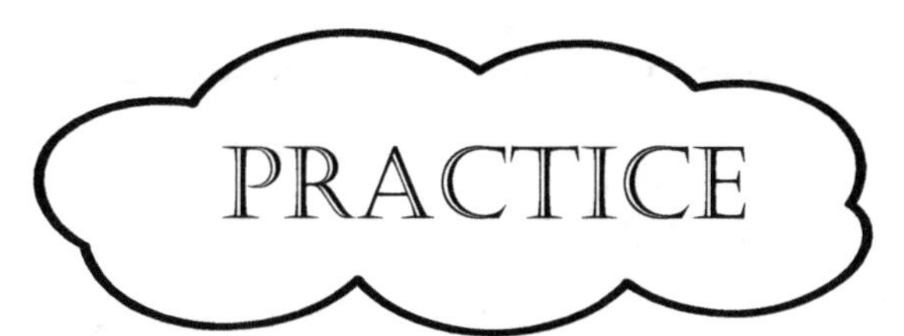
PRACTICE

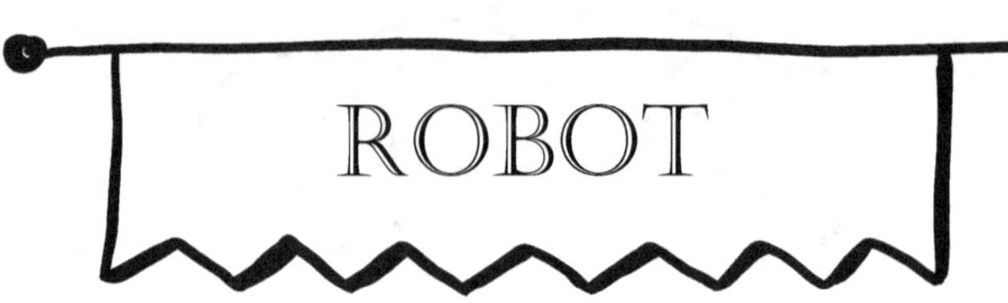

Step 1

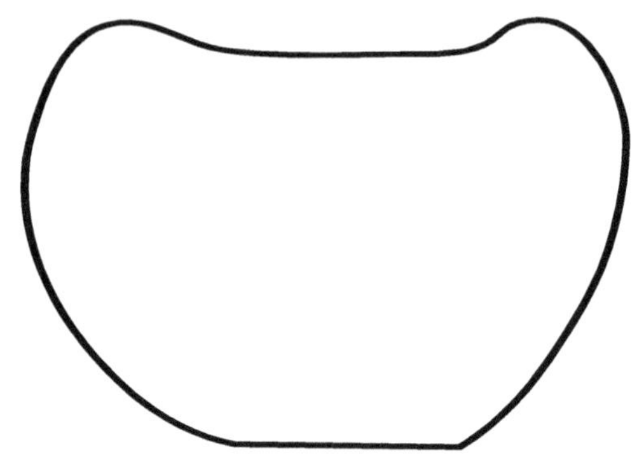

Step 2

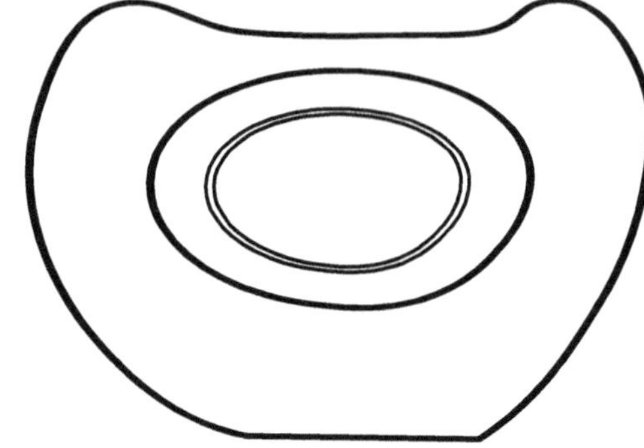

Step 3

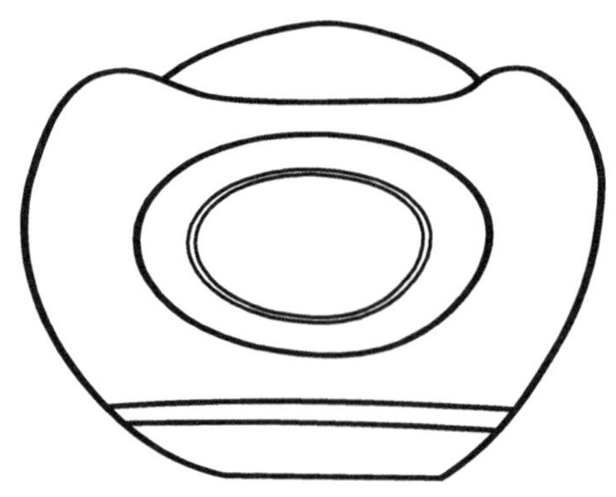

Step 4

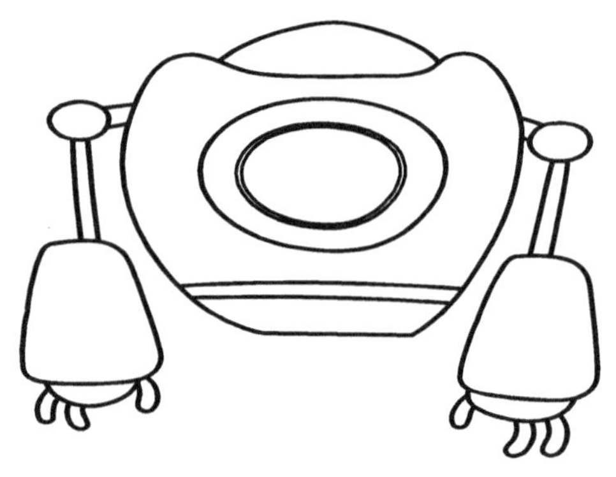

Step 5

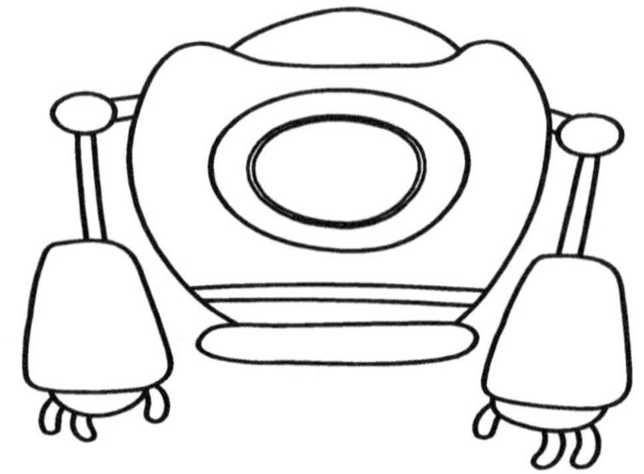

Step 6

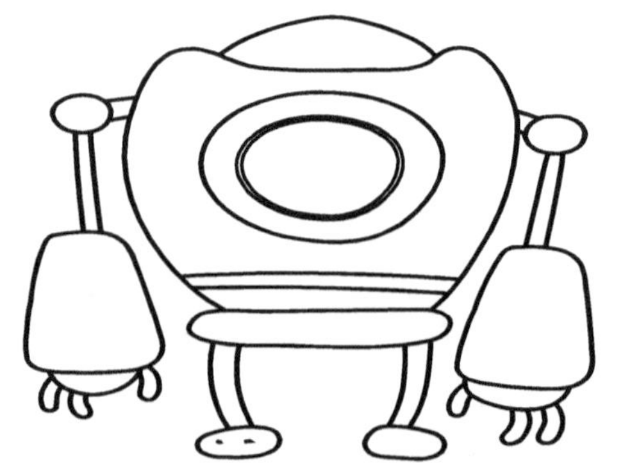

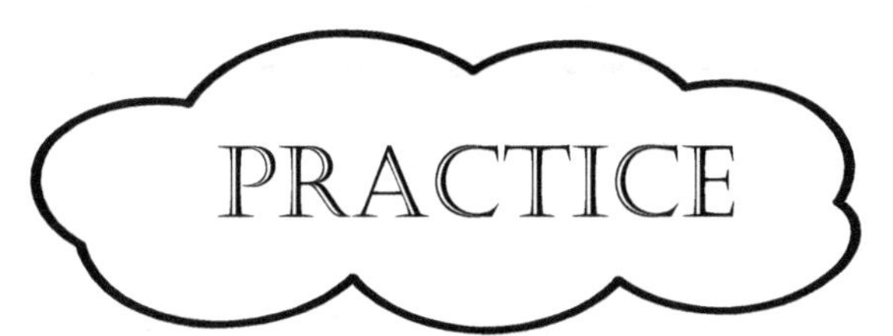
PRACTICE

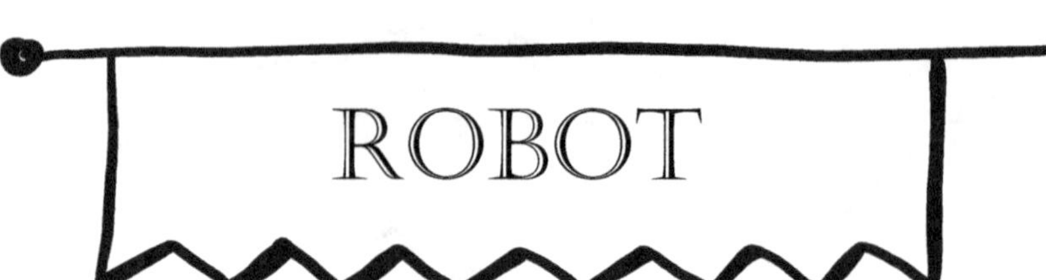

Step 1

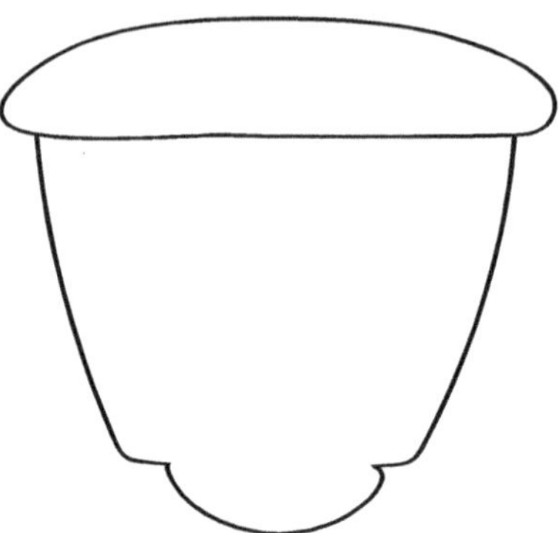

Step 2

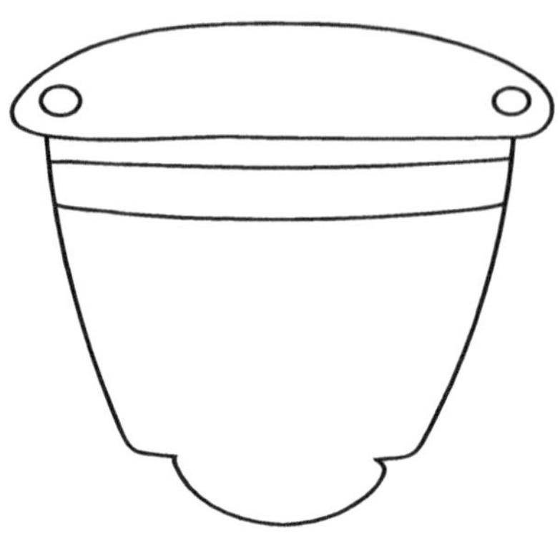

Step 3

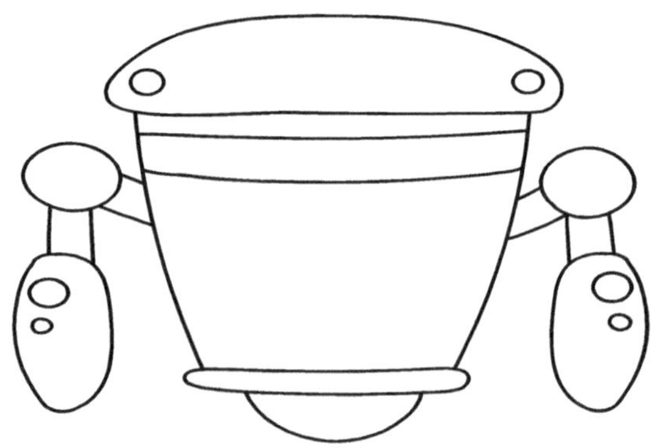

Step 4

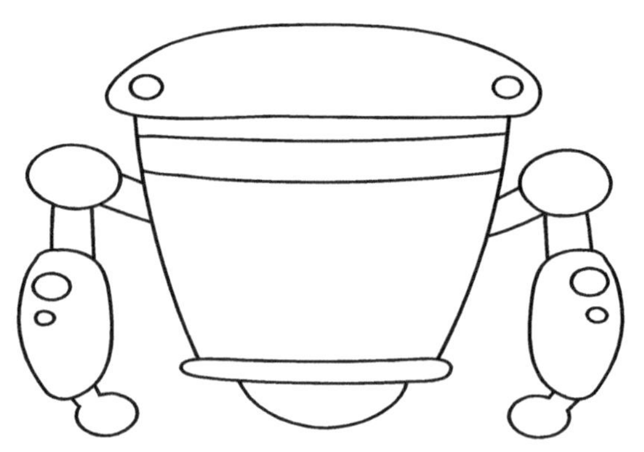

Step 5

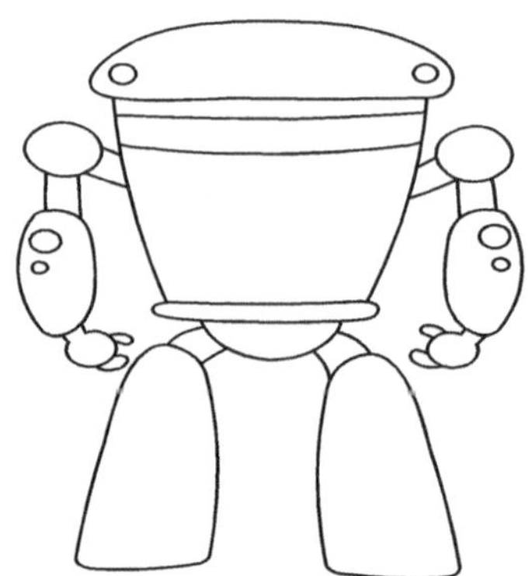

Step 6

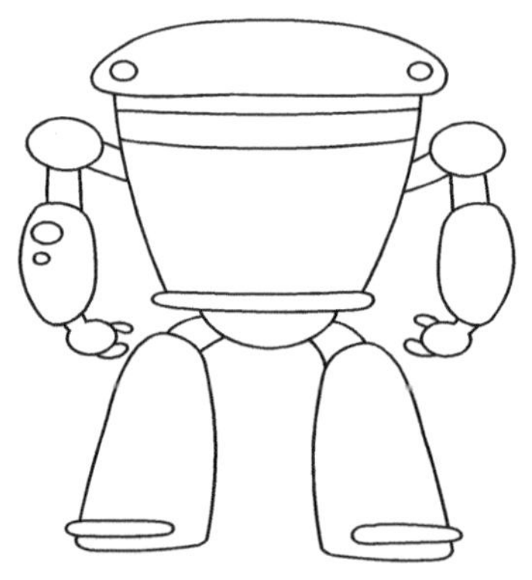

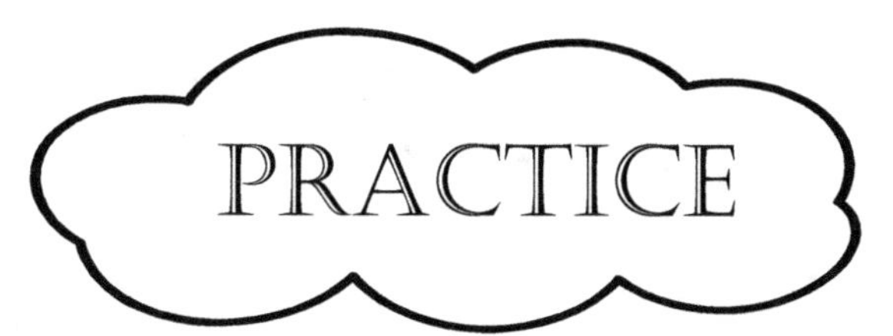
PRACTICE

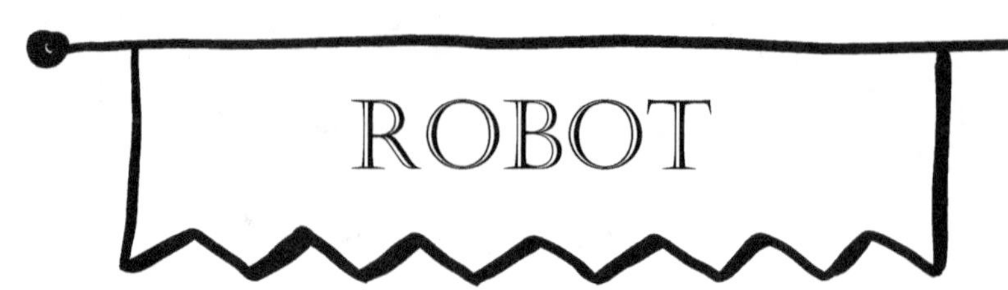

Step 1

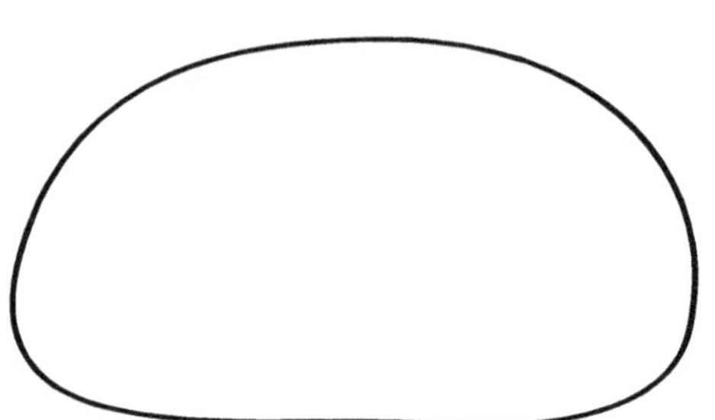

Step 2

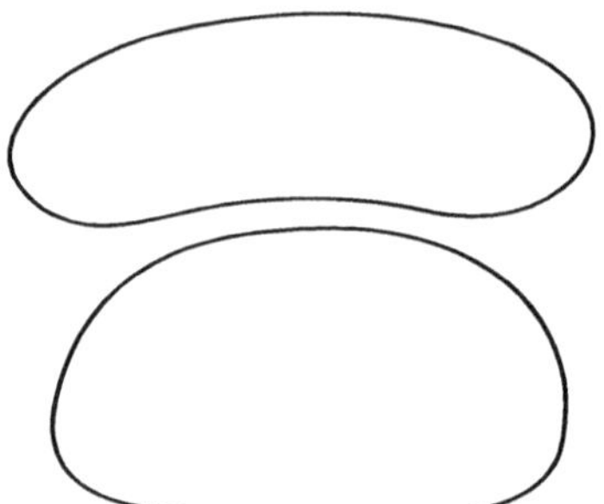

Step 3

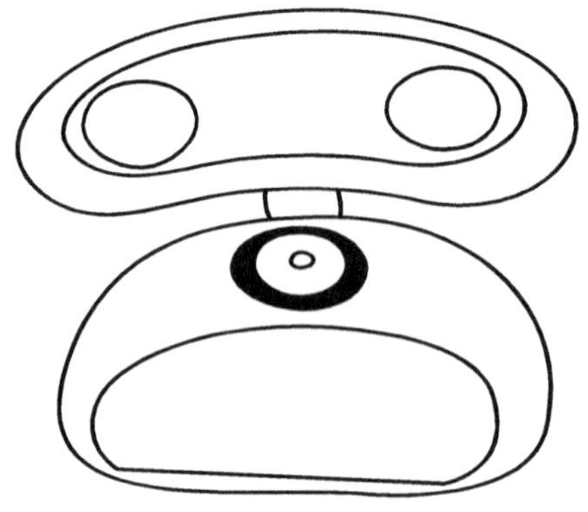

Step 4

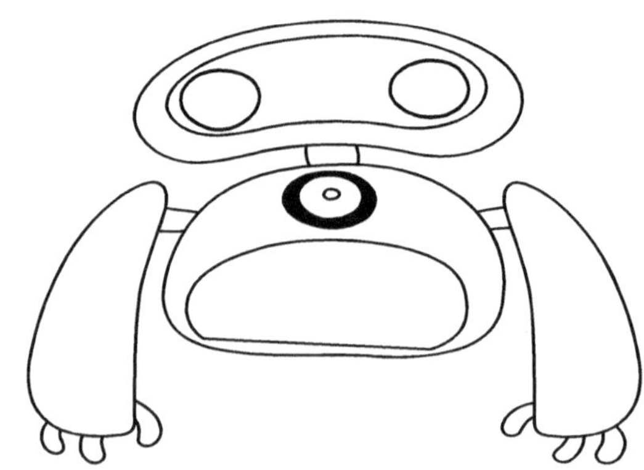

Step 5

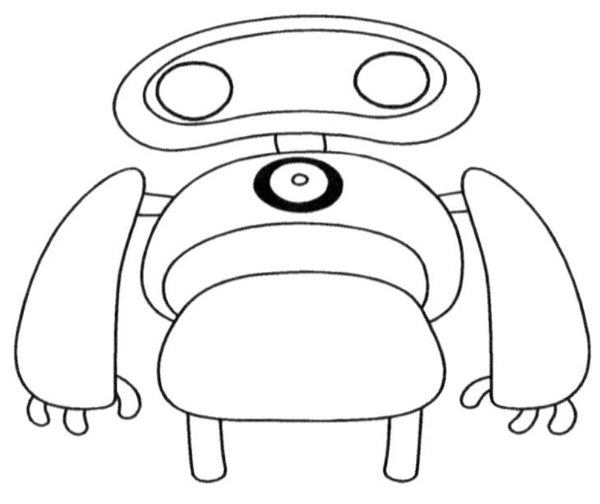

Step 6

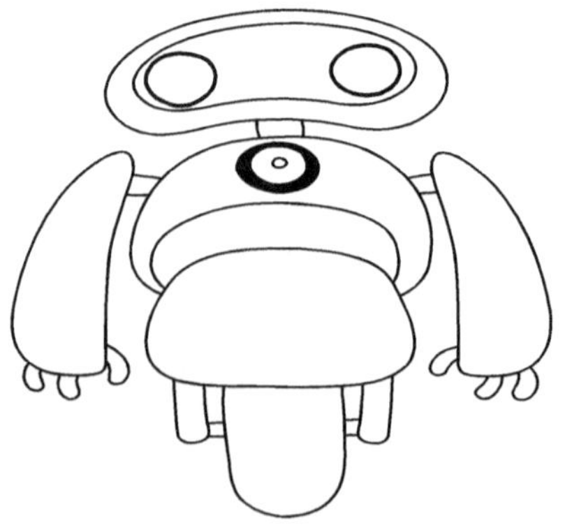

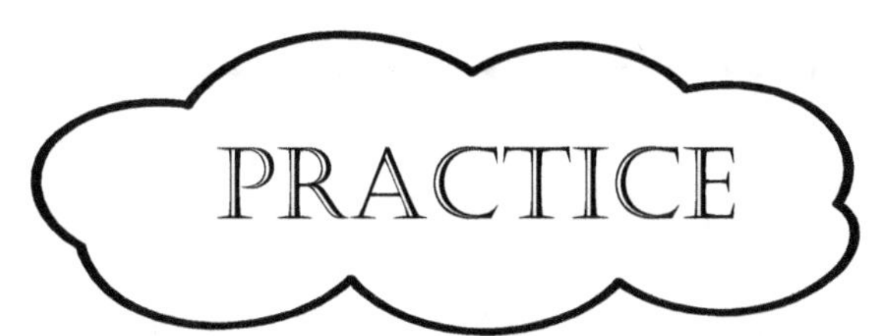
PRACTICE

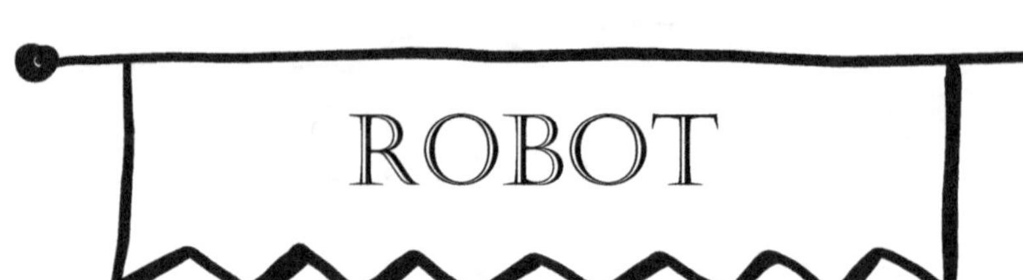

Step 1

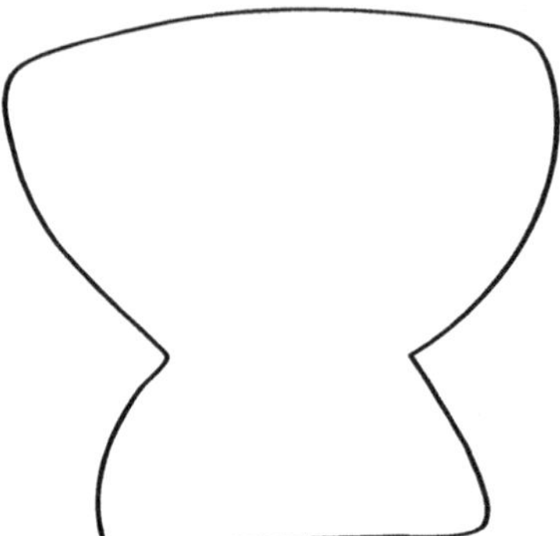

Step 2

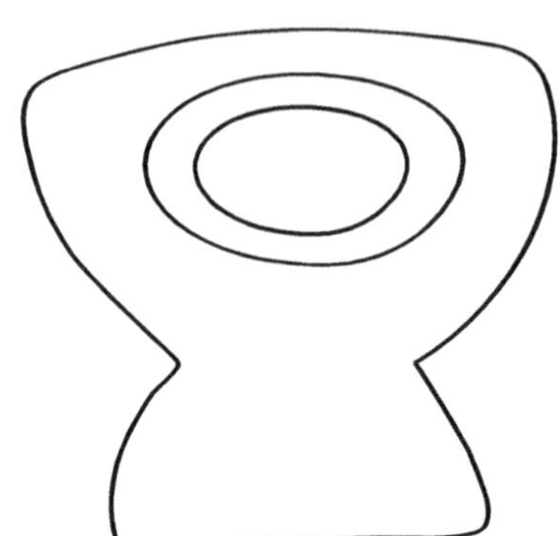

Step 3

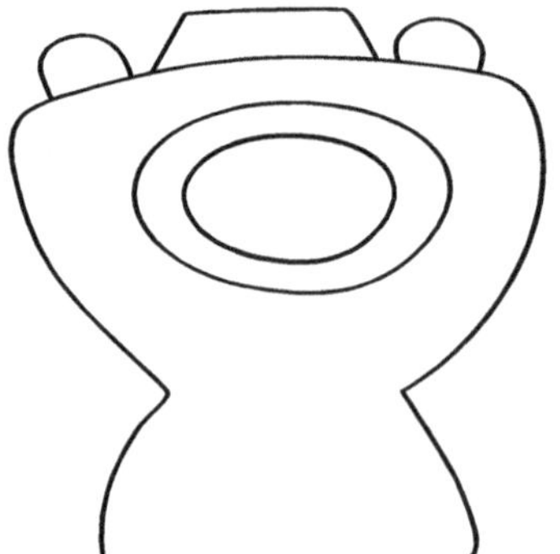

Step 4

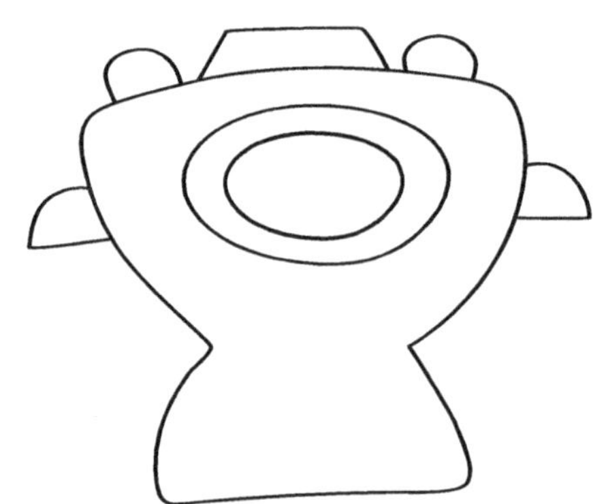

Step 5

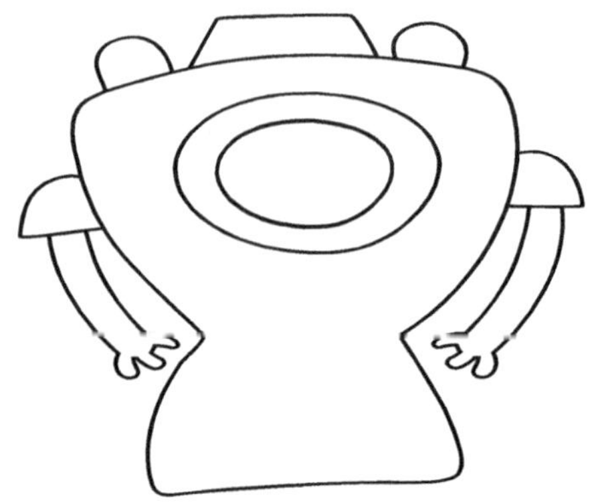

Step 6

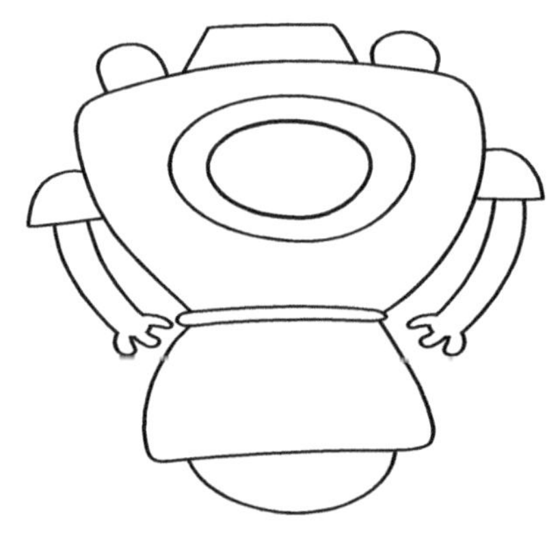

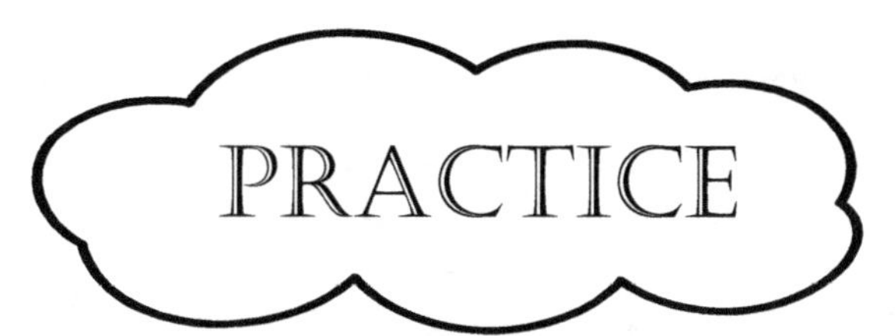
PRACTICE

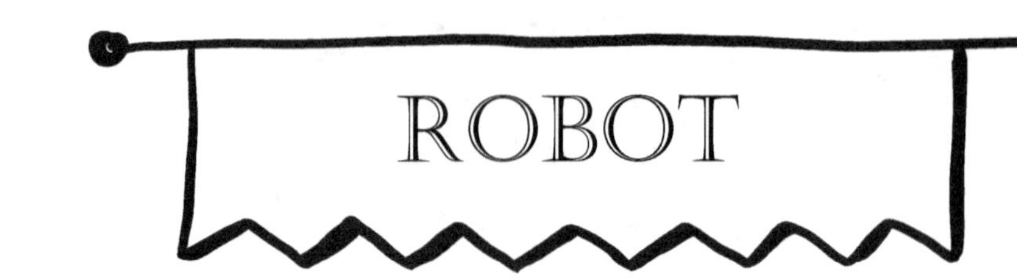

Step 1

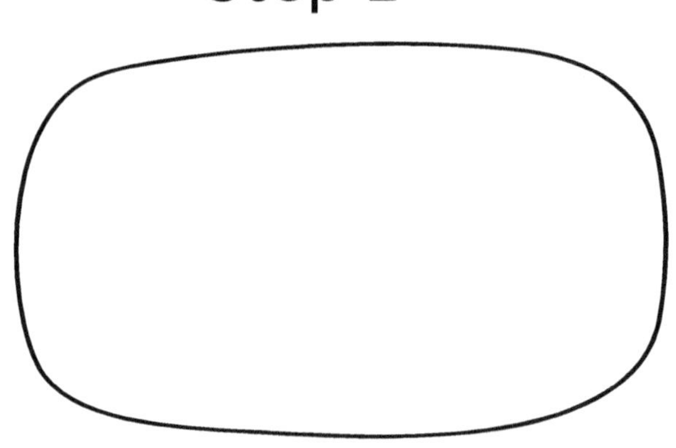

Step 2

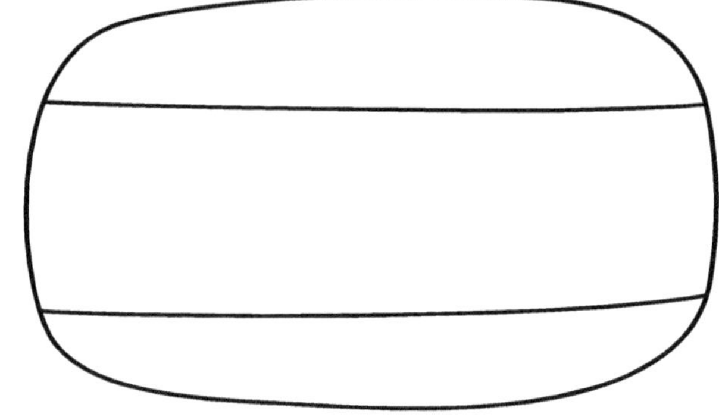

Step 3

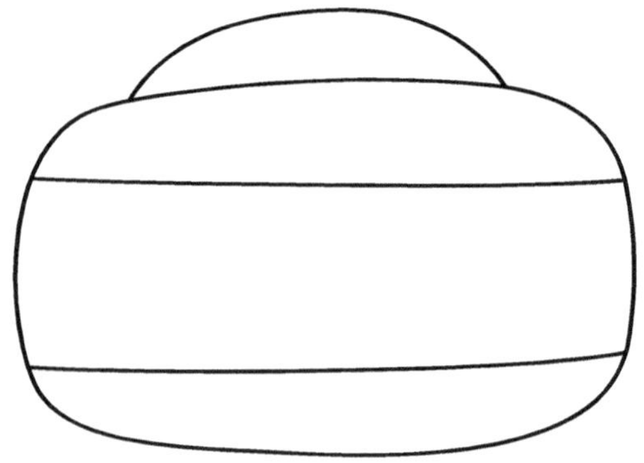

Step 4

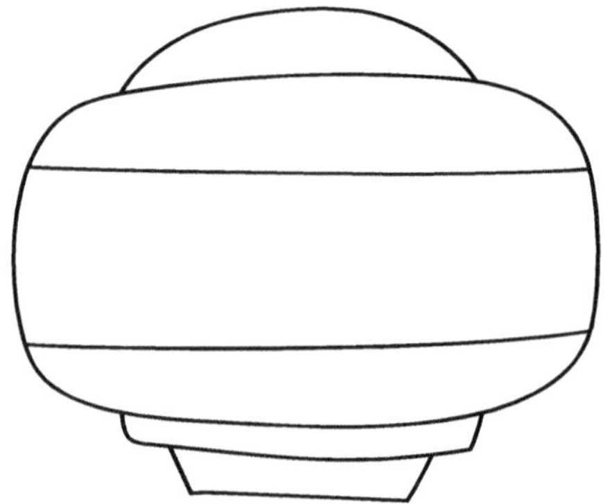

Step 5

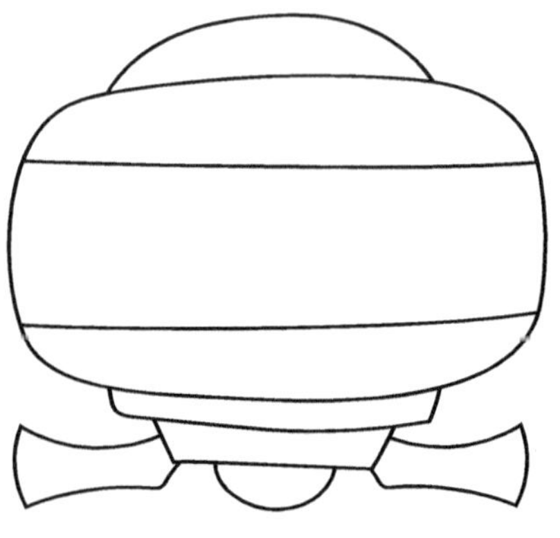

Step 6

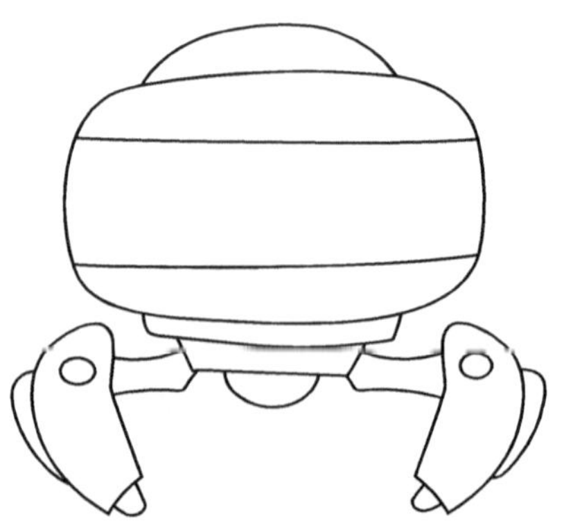

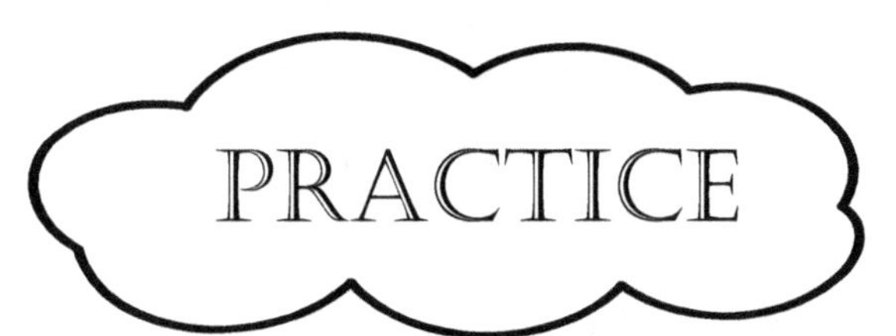
PRACTICE

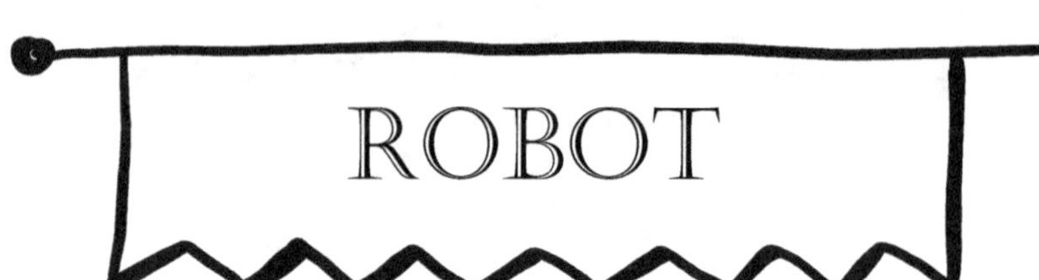

Step 1

Step 2

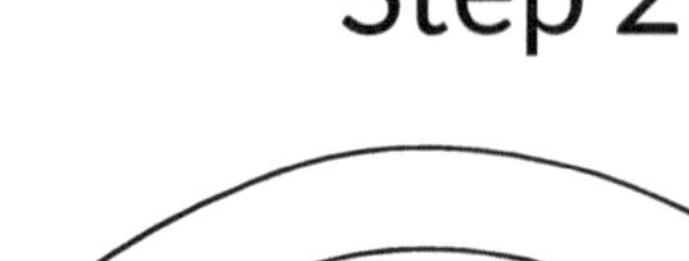

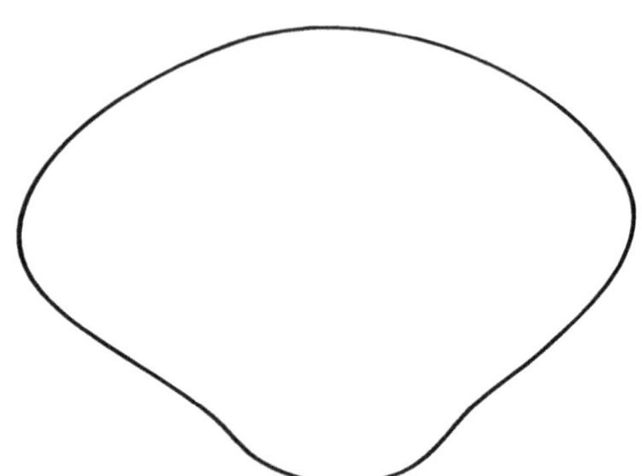

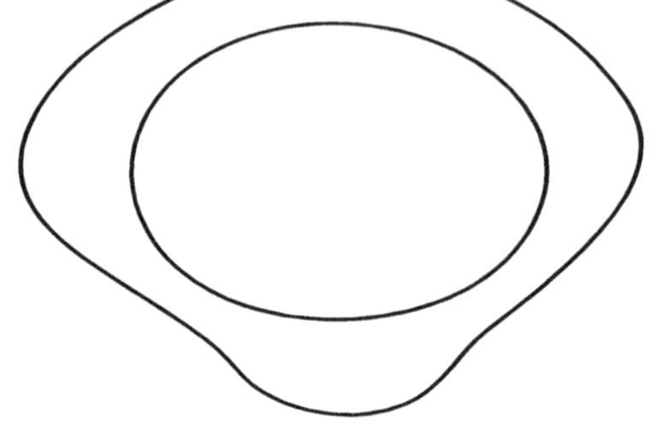

Step 3

Step 4

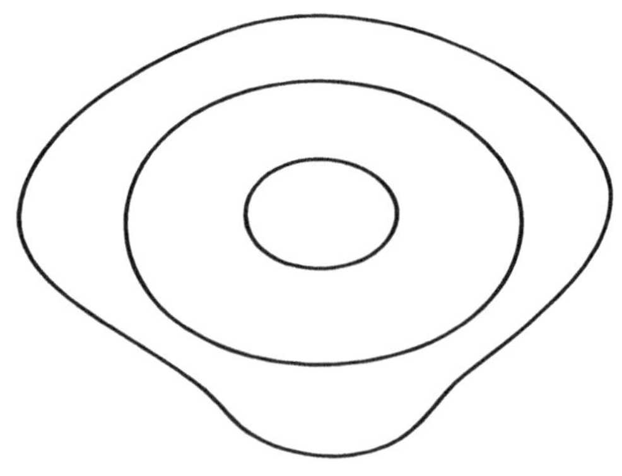

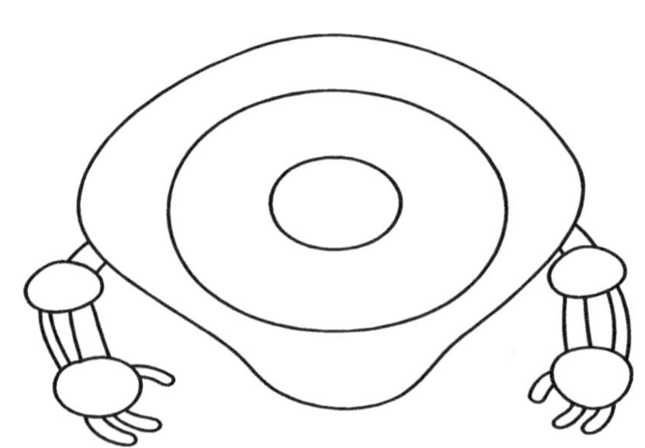

Step 5

Step 6

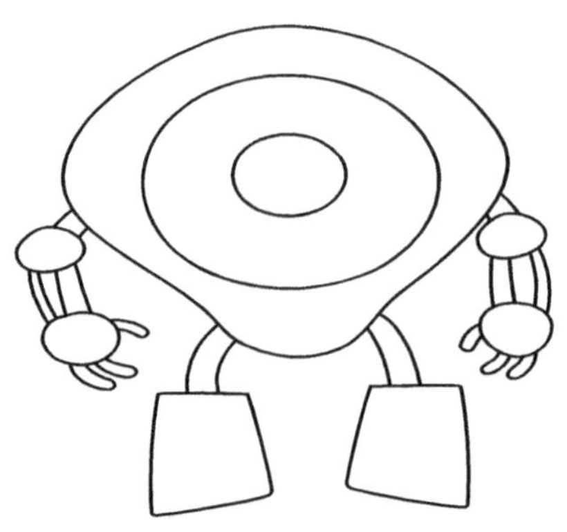

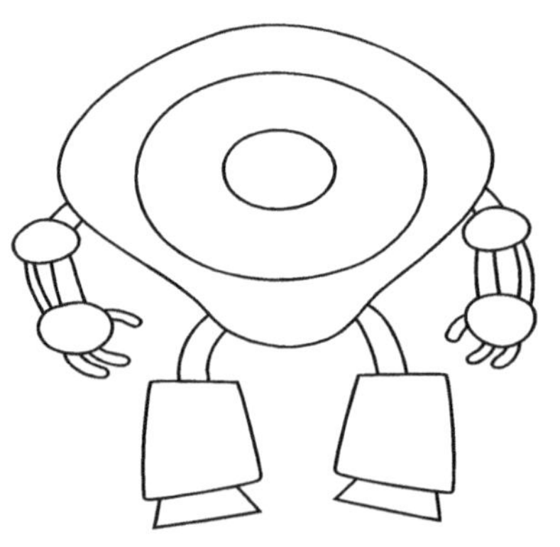

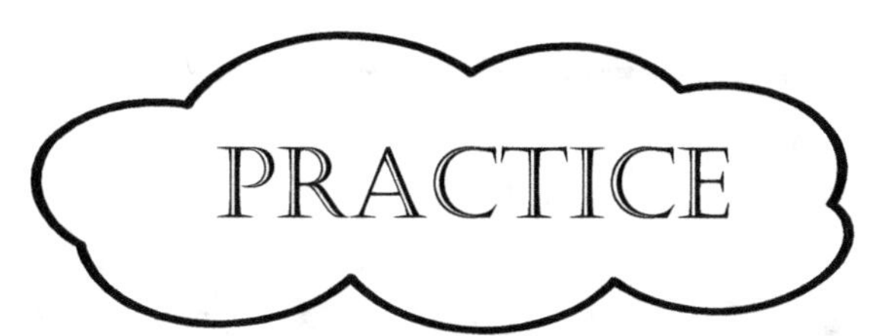
PRACTICE

ROBOT

Step 1

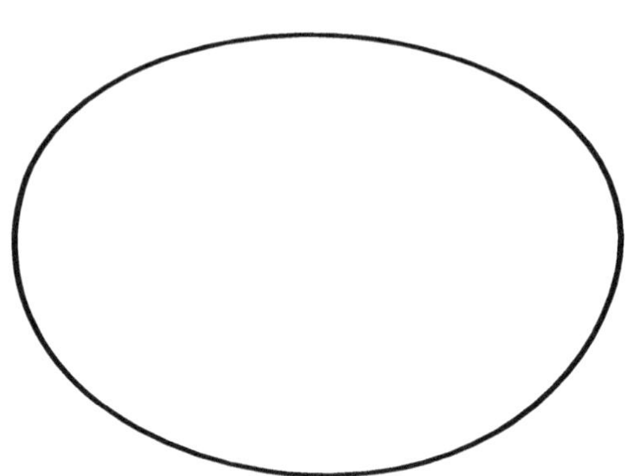

Step 2

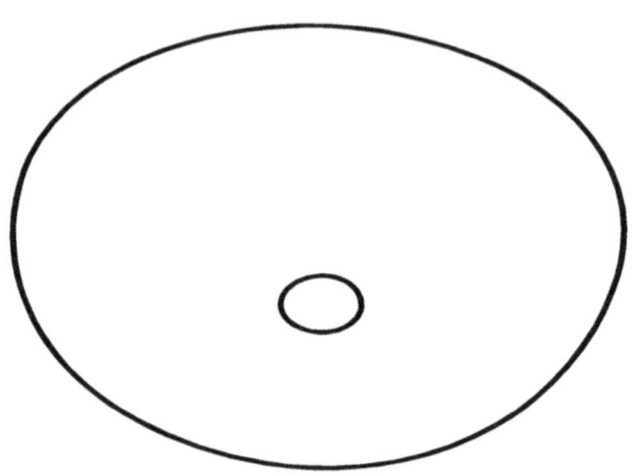

Step 3

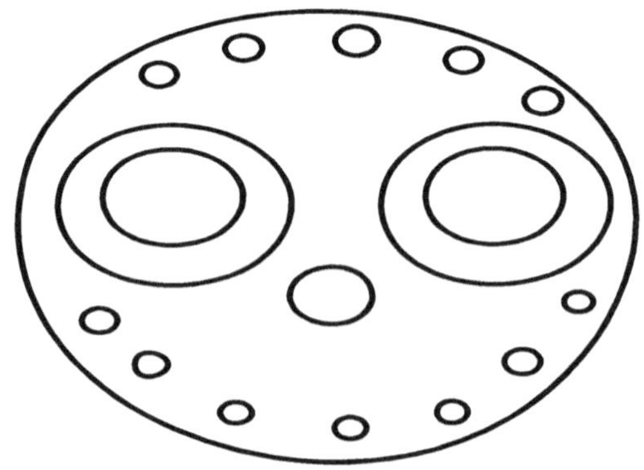

Step 4

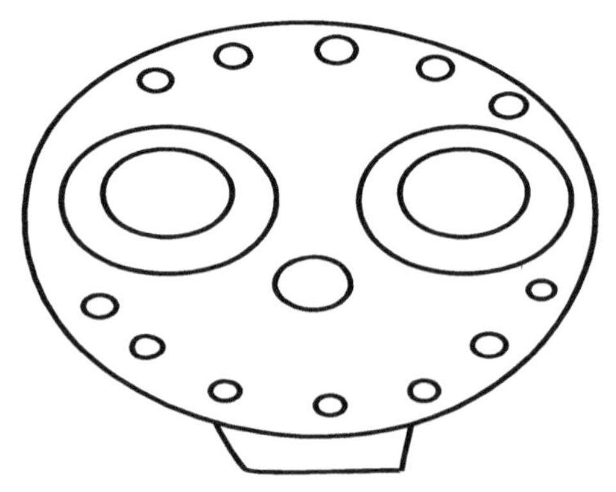

Step 5

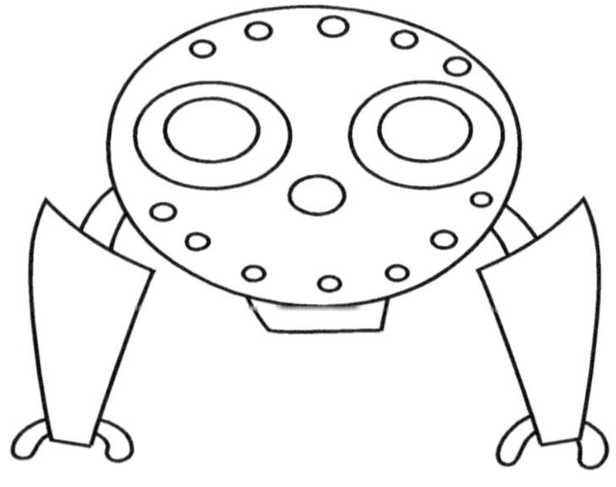

Step 6

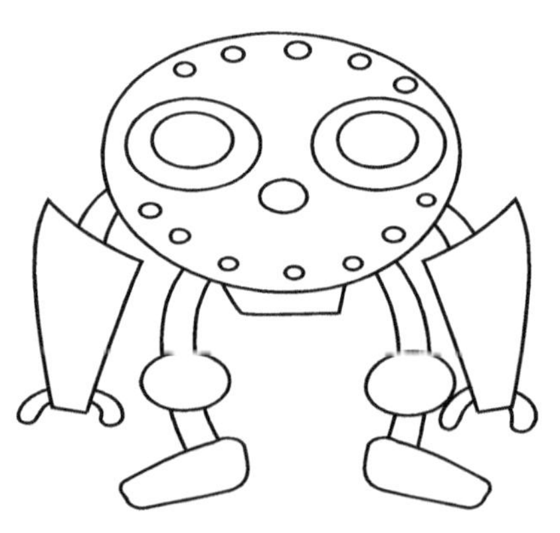

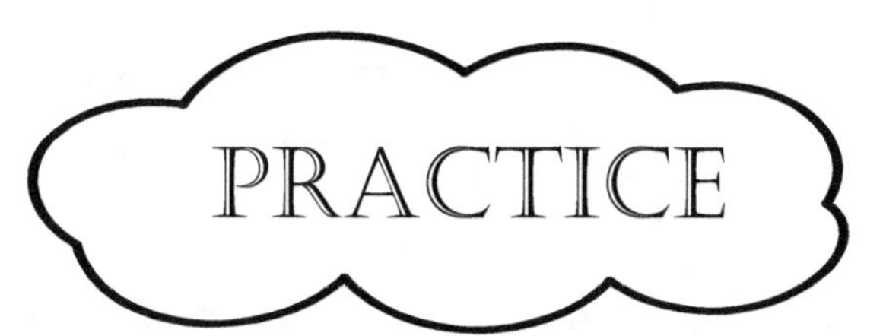
PRACTICE

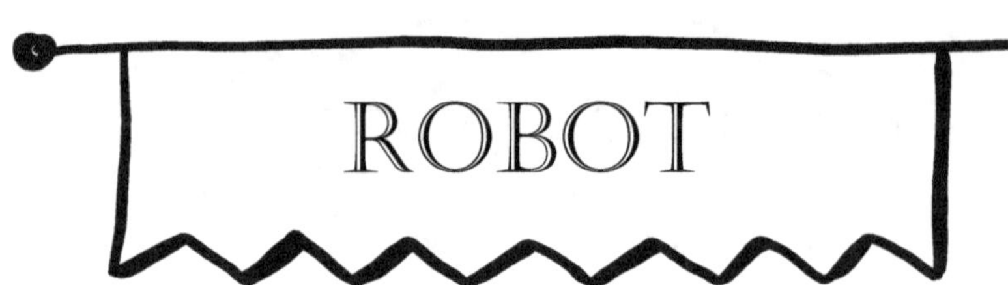

Step 1

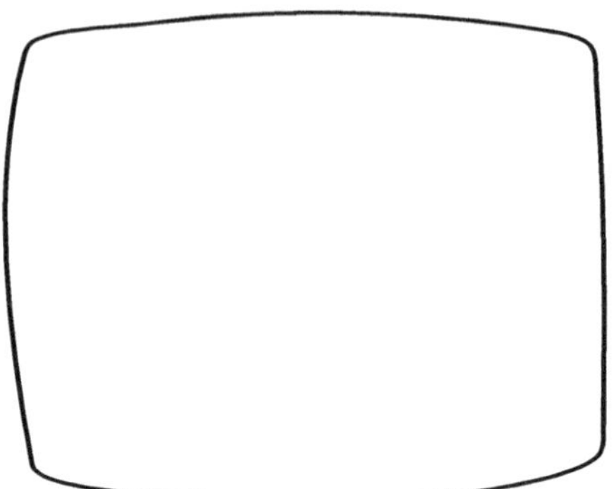

Step 2

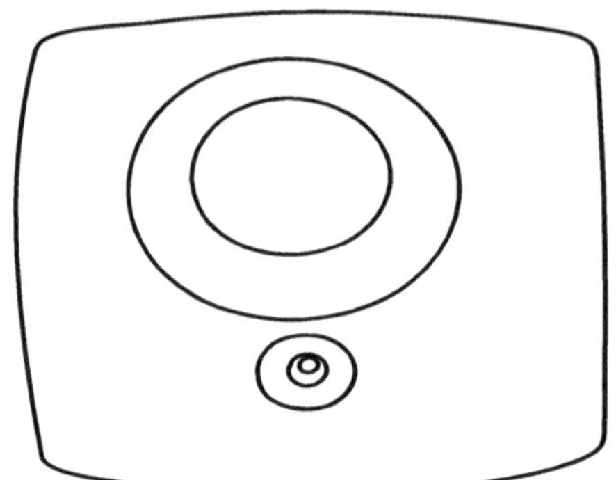

Step 3

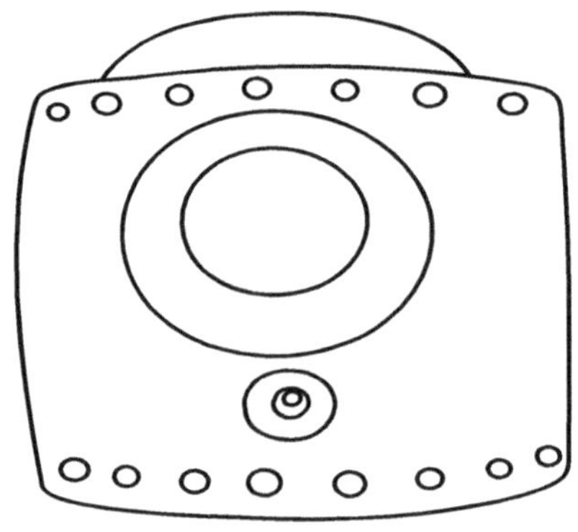

Step 4

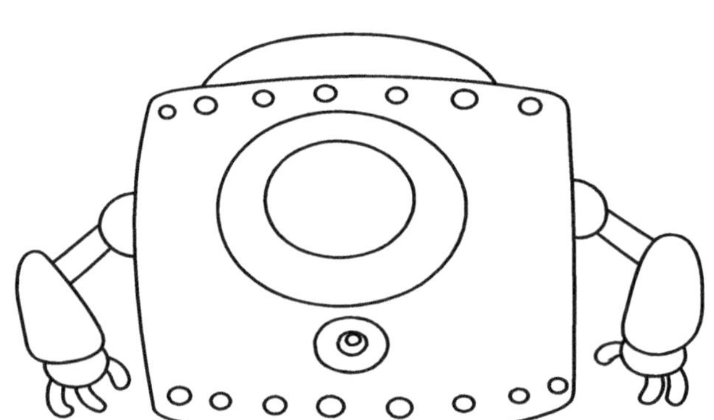

Step 5

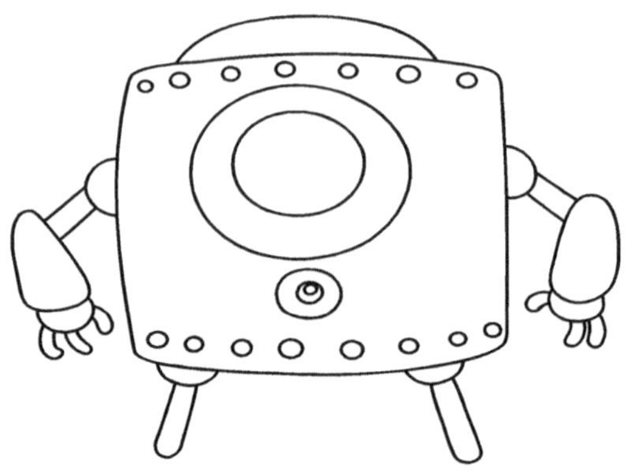

Step 6

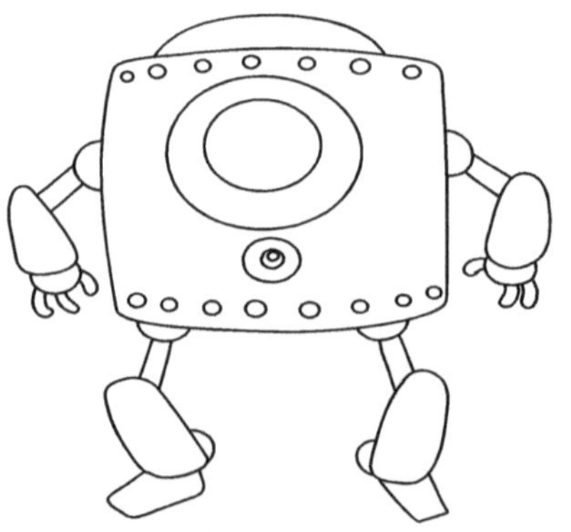

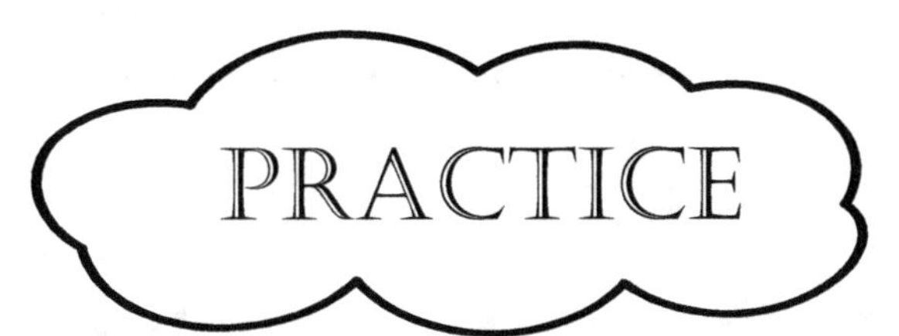
PRACTICE

ROBOT

Step 1

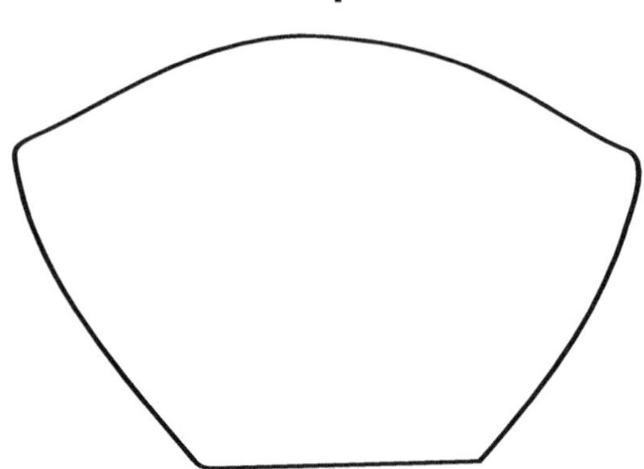

Step 2

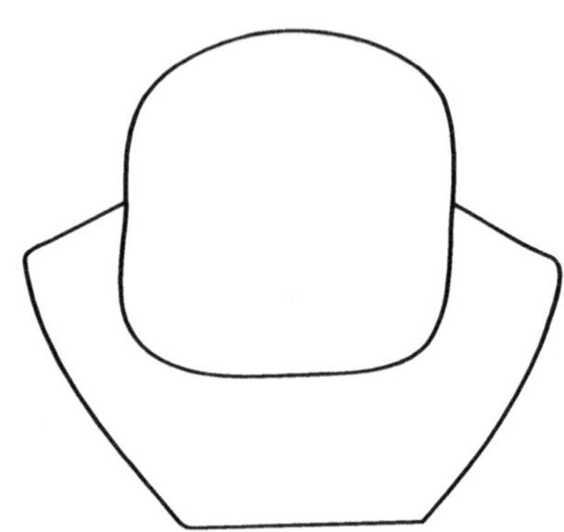

Step 3

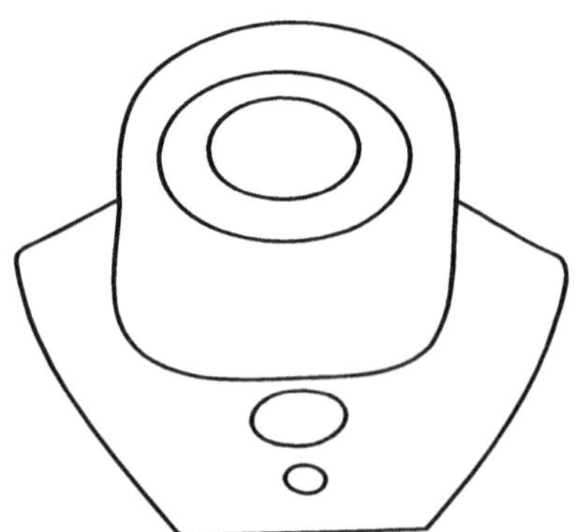

Step 4

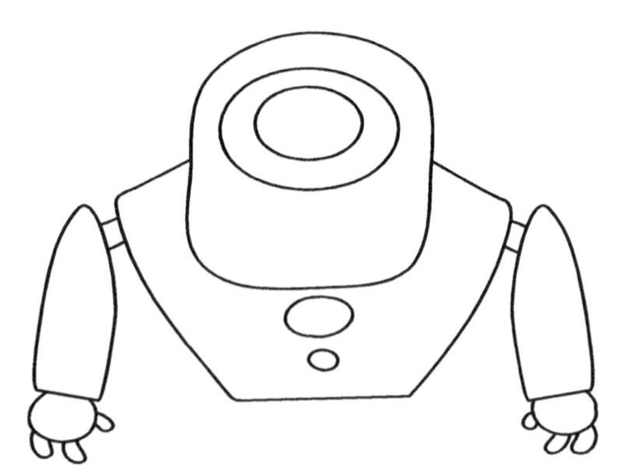

Step 5

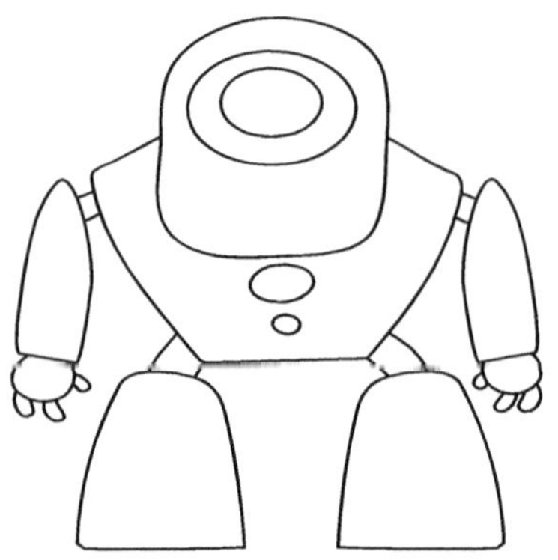

Step 6

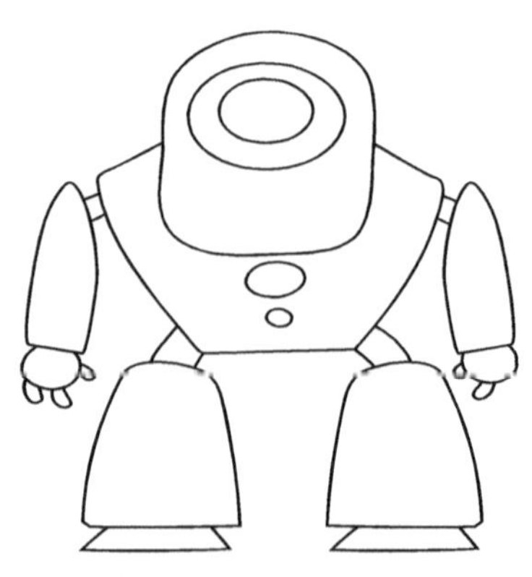

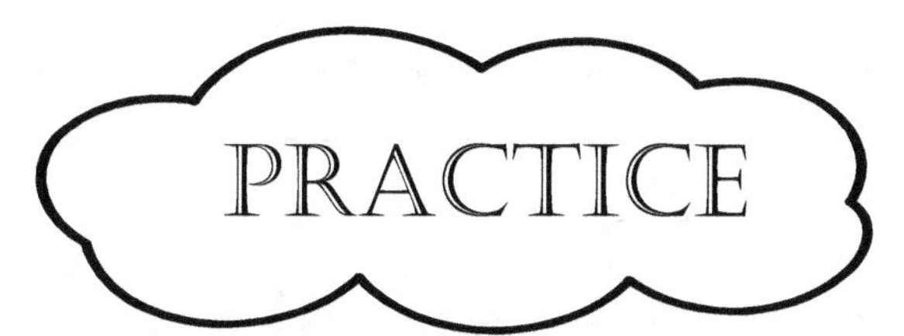
PRACTICE

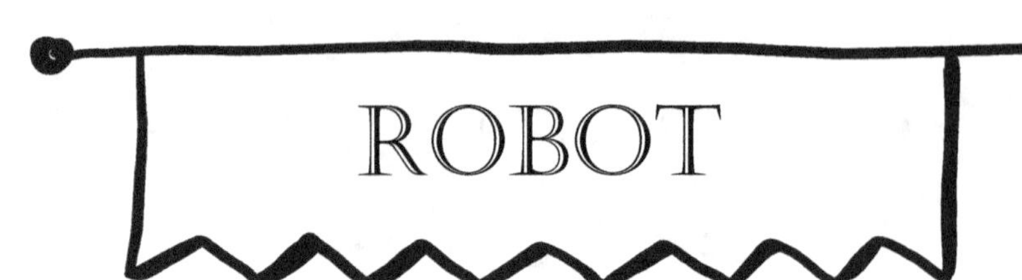

Step 1

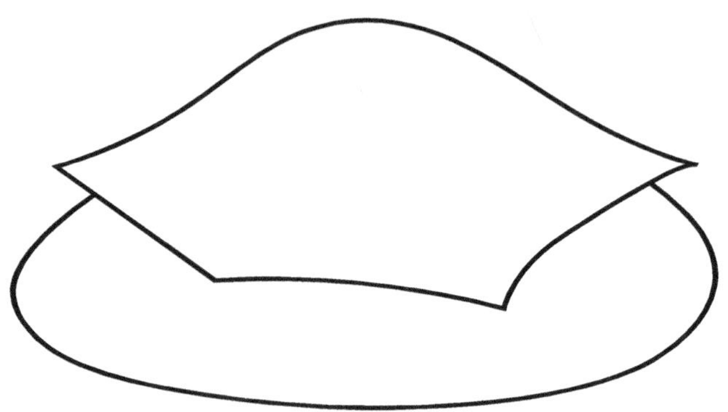

Step 2

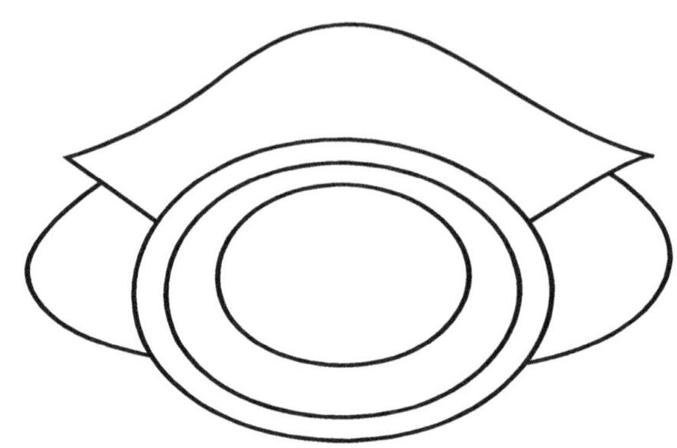

Step 3

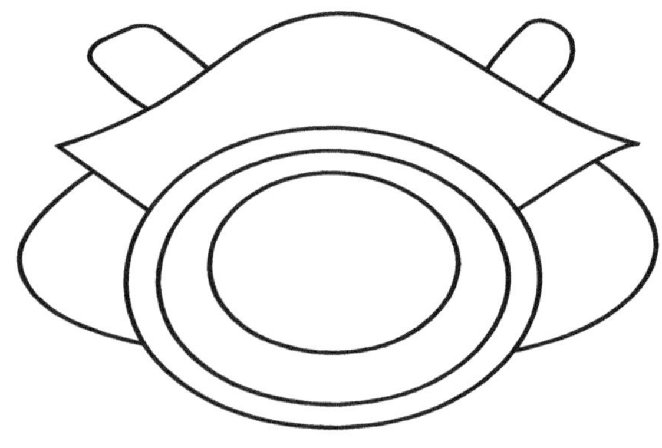

Step 4

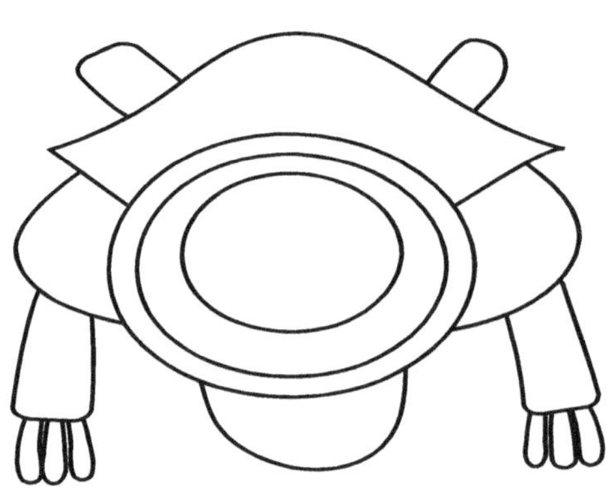

Step 5

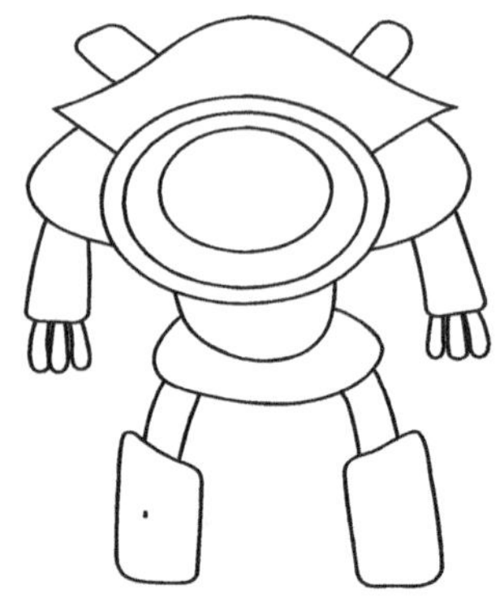

Step 6

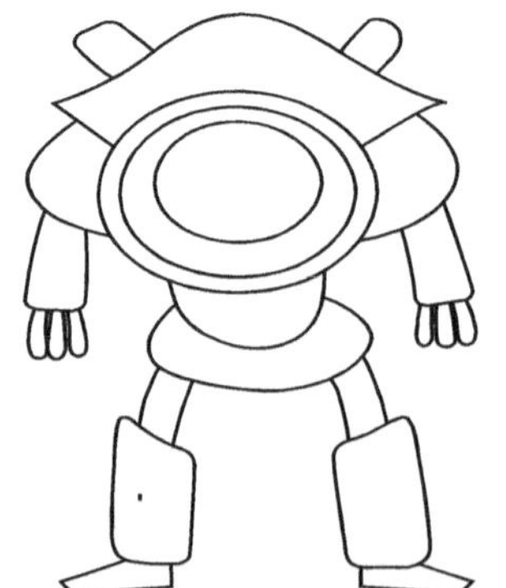

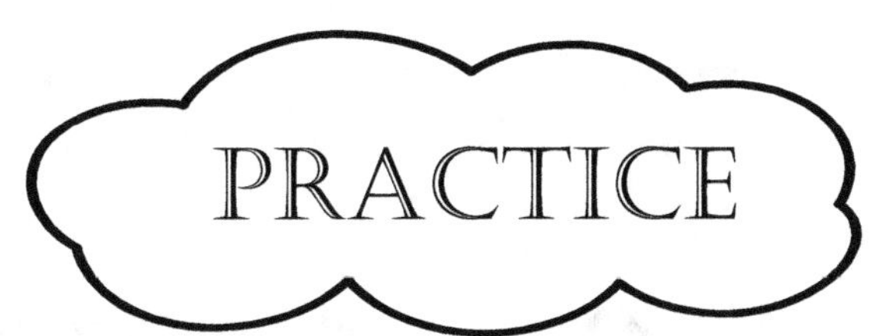
PRACTICE

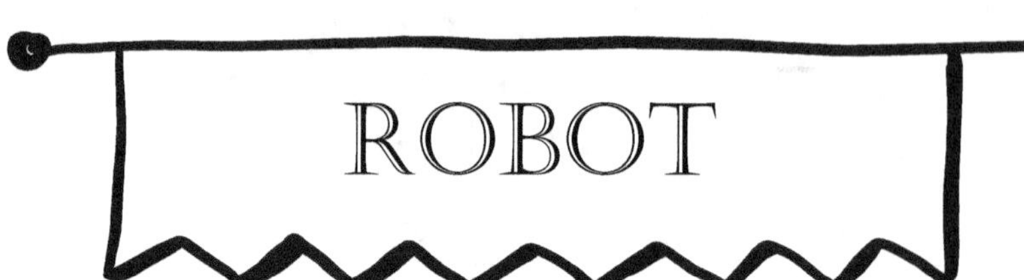

Step 1

Step 2

Step 3

Step 4

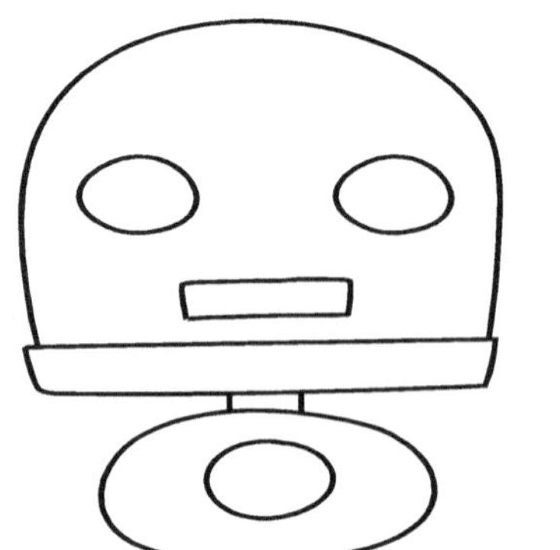

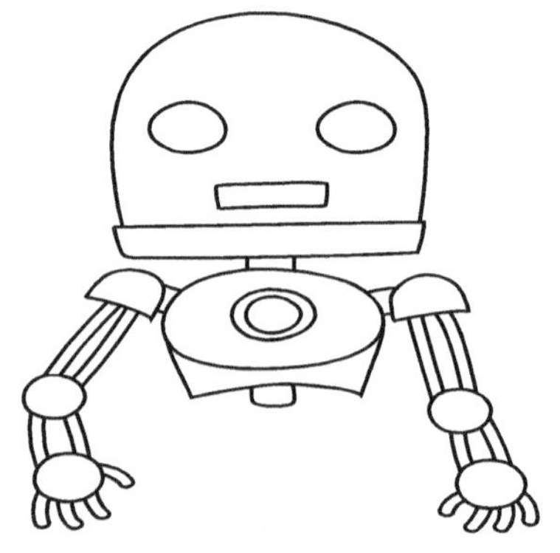

Step 5

Step 6

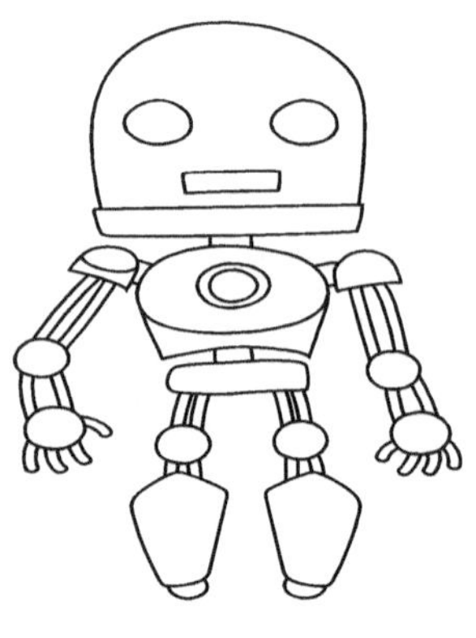

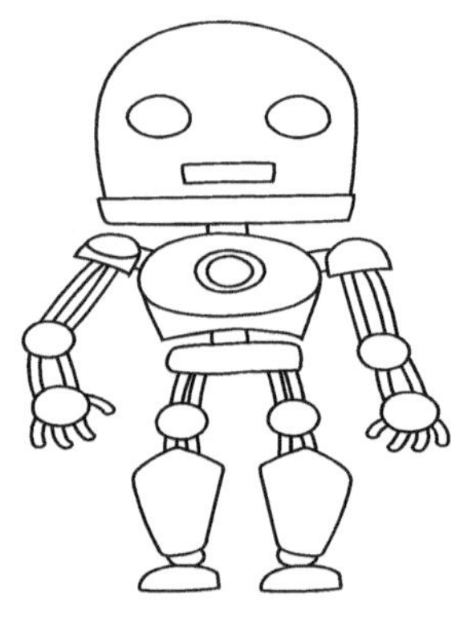

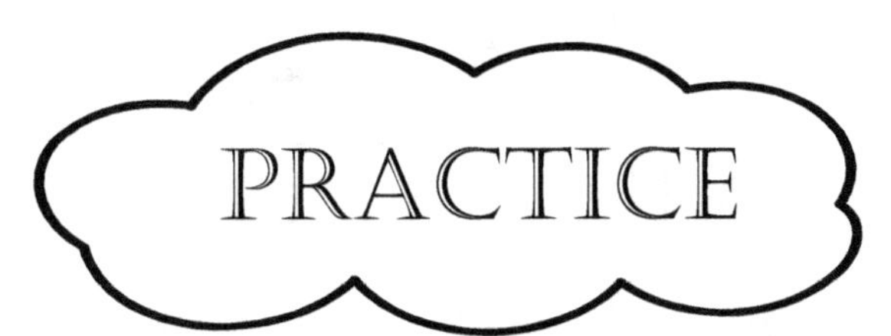
PRACTICE

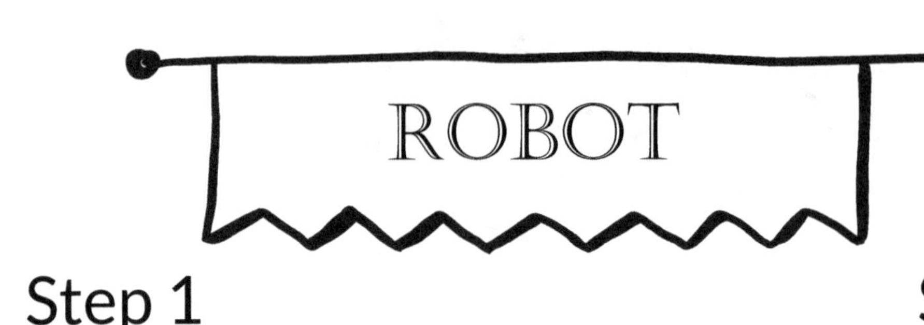

Step 1

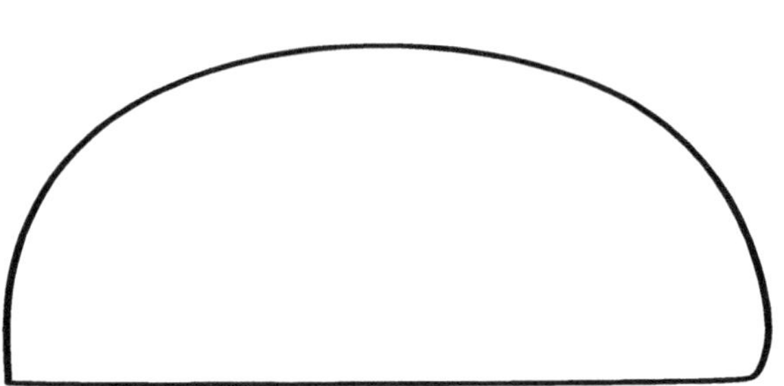

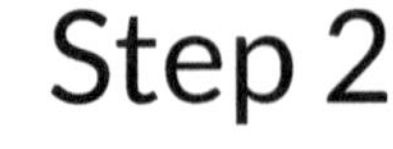

Step 2

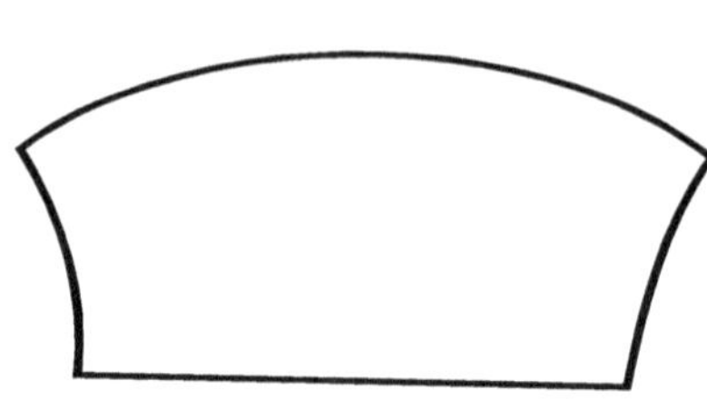

Step 3

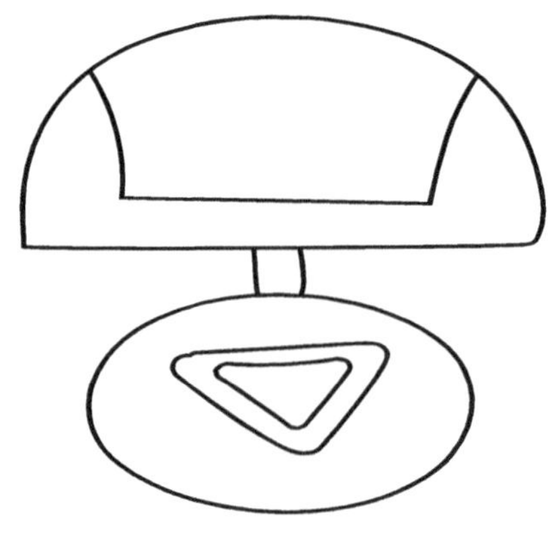

Step 4

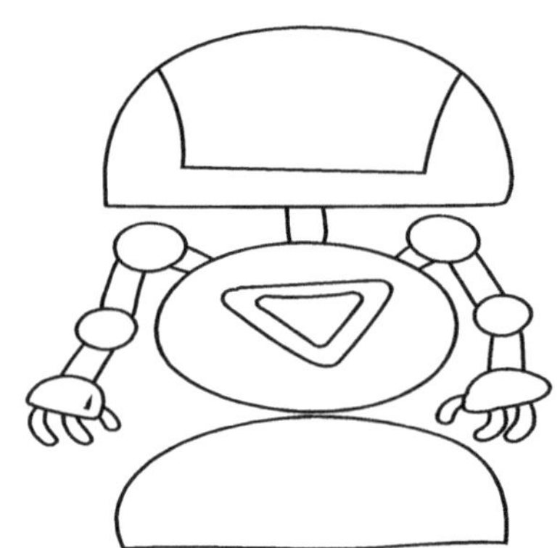

Step 5

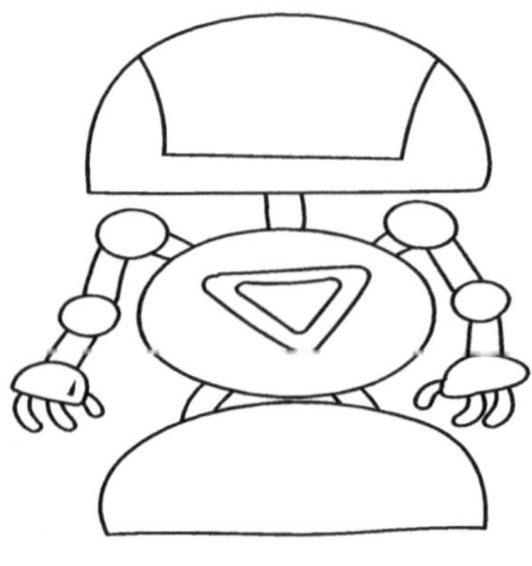

Step 6

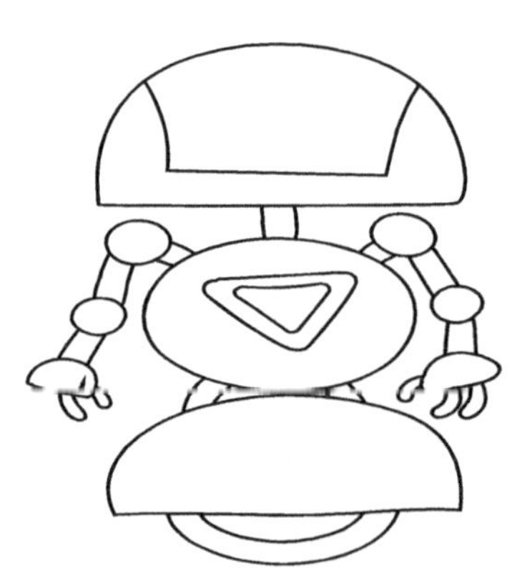

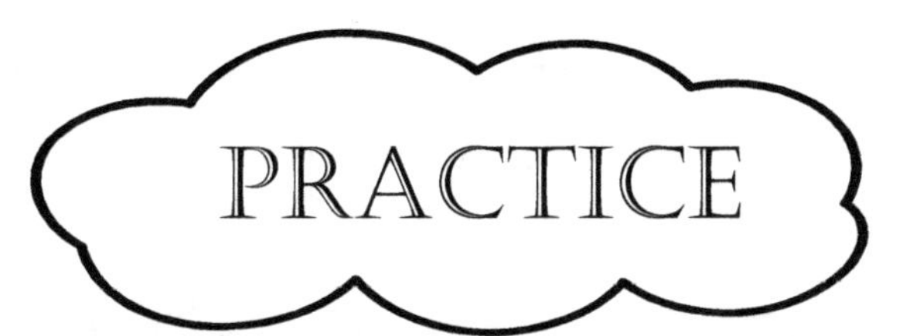
PRACTICE

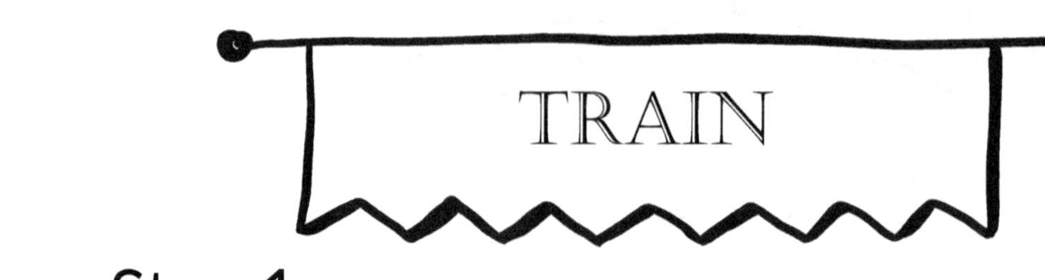

Step 1

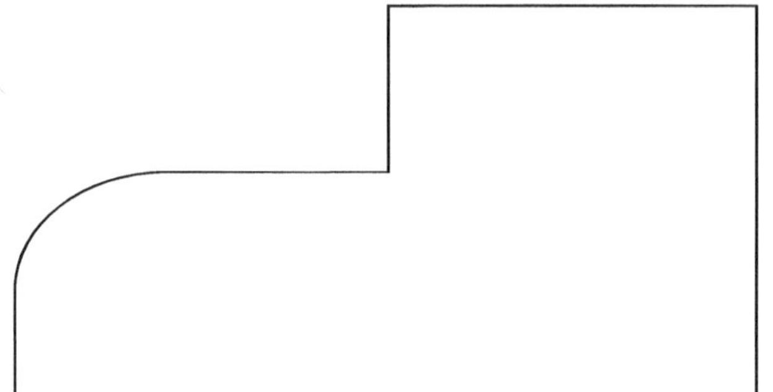

Step 2

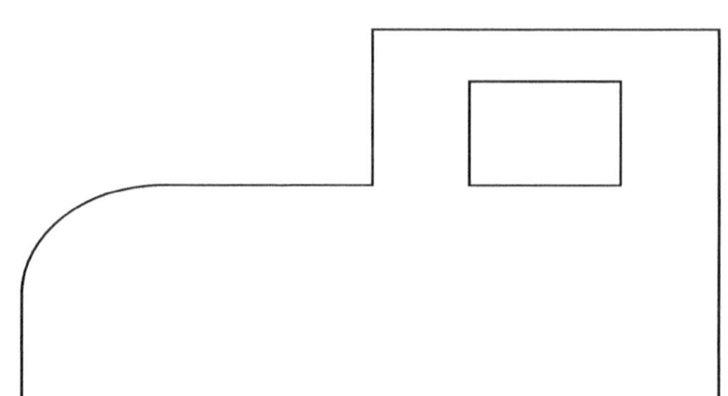

Step 3

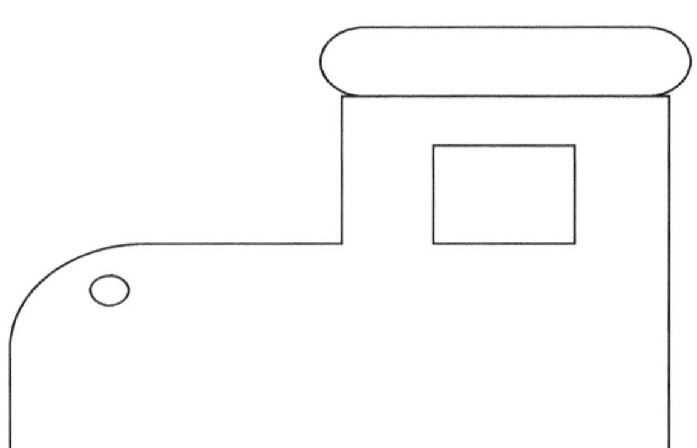

Step 4

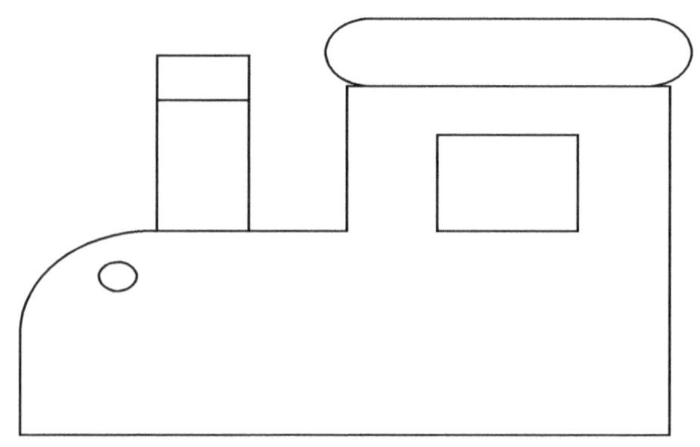

Step 5

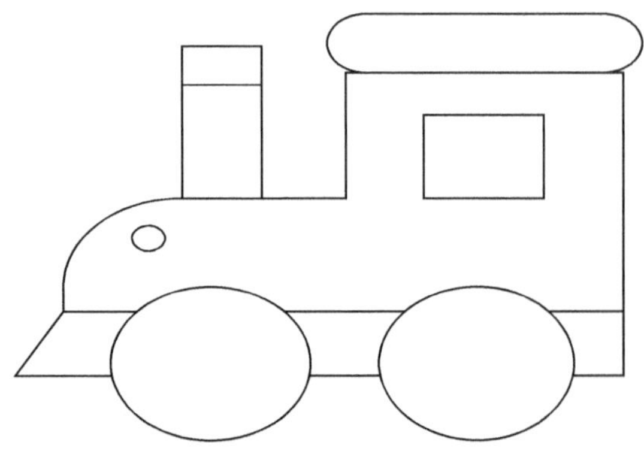

Step 6

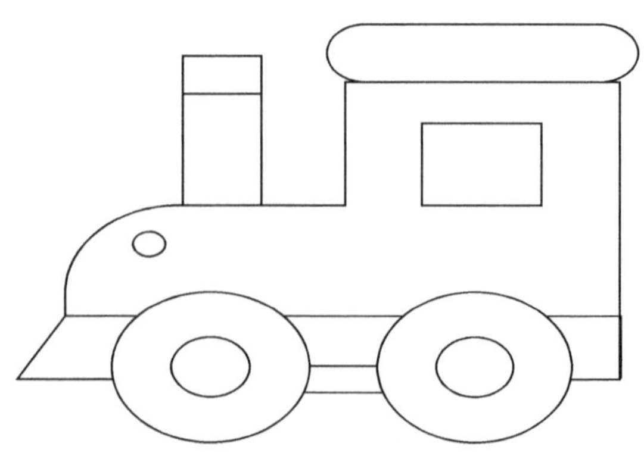

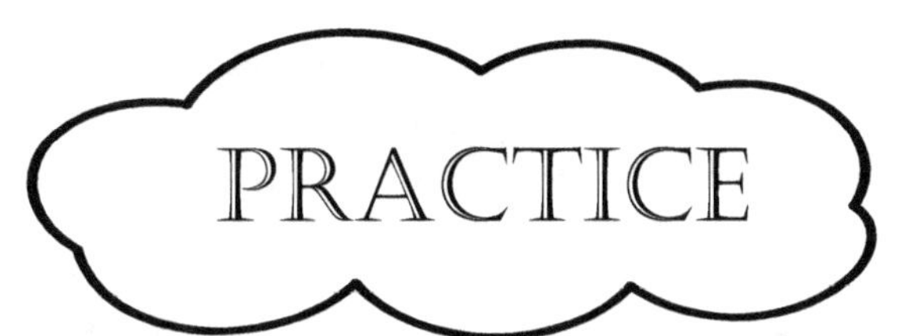
PRACTICE

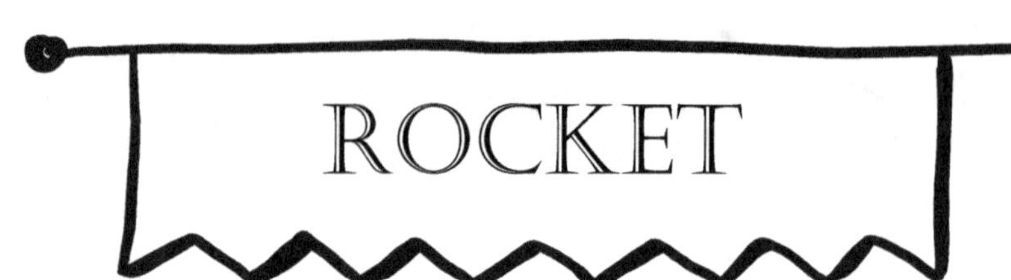

Step 1

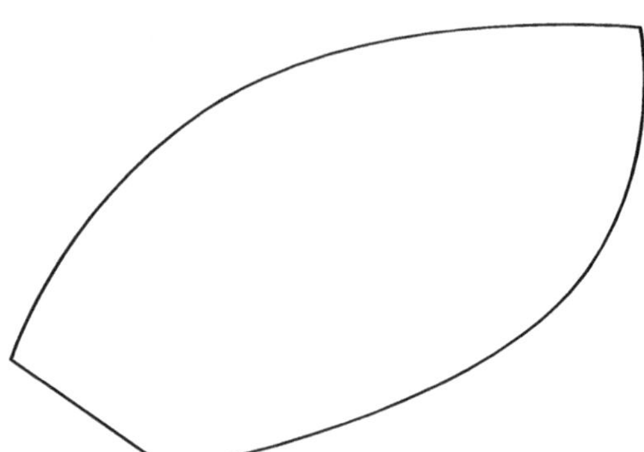
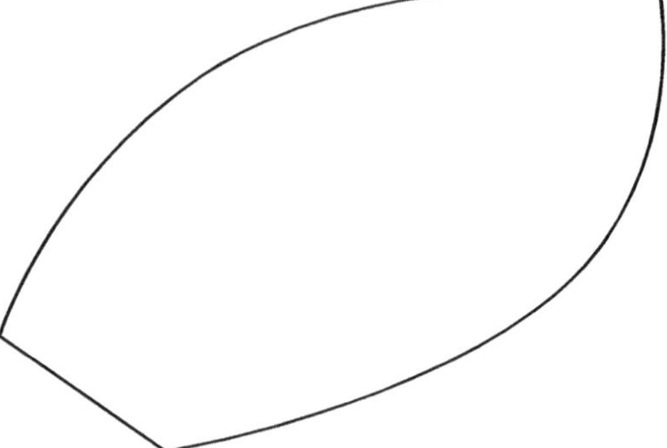

Step 2

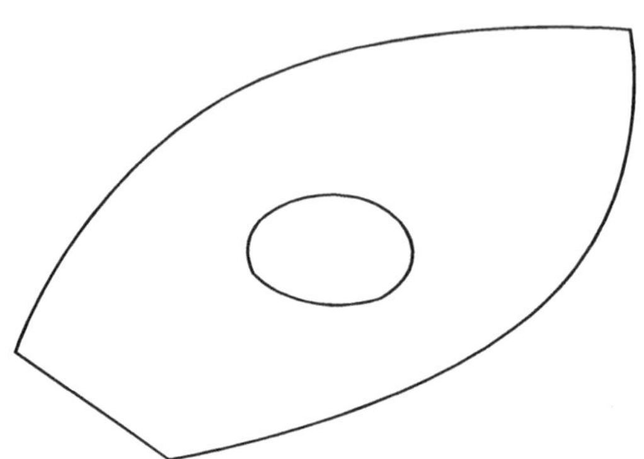

Step 3

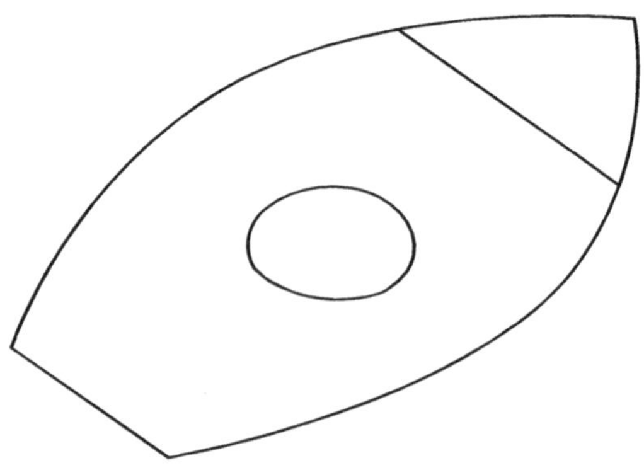
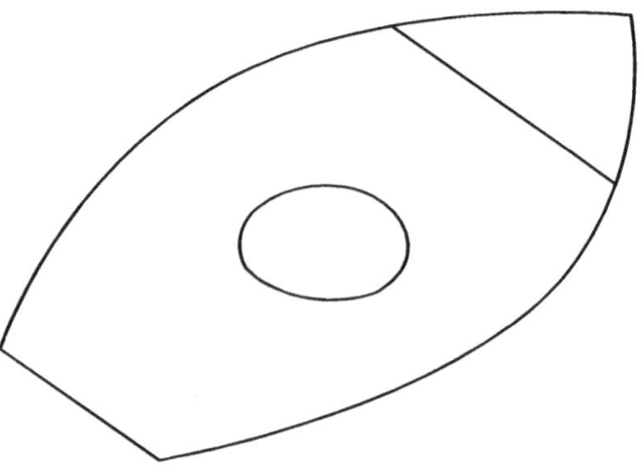

Step 4

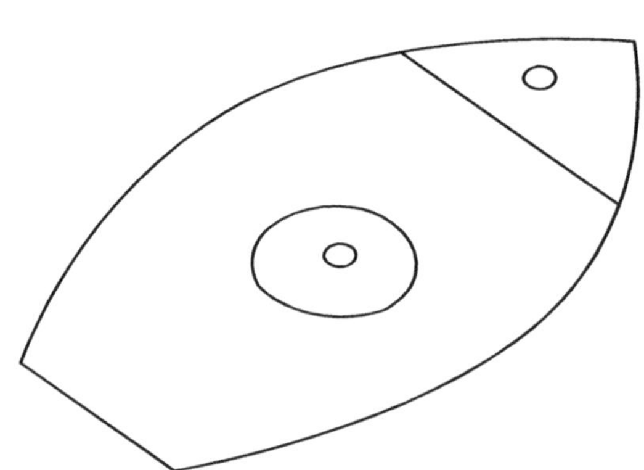

Step 5

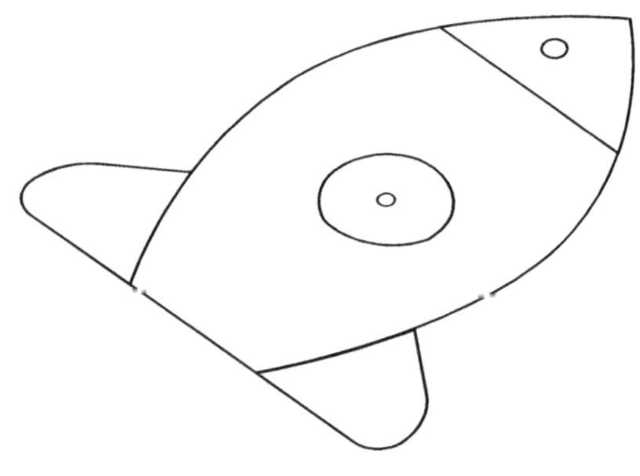

Step 6

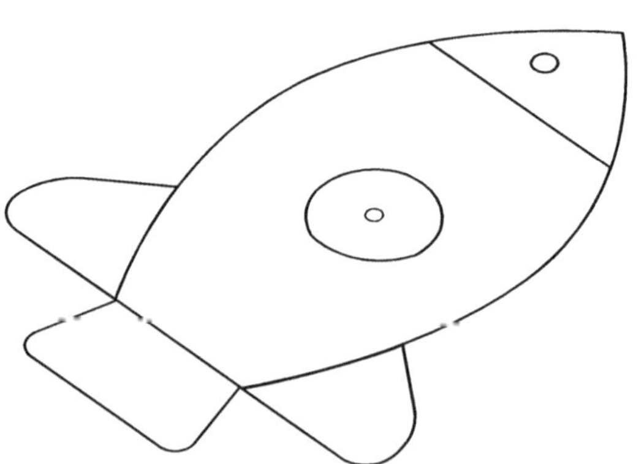

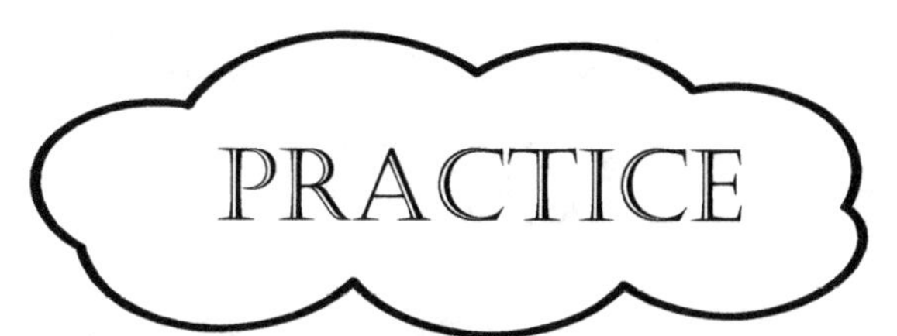
PRACTICE

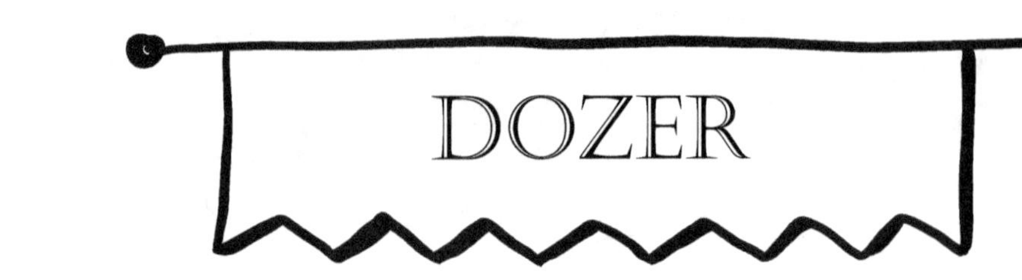

Step 1

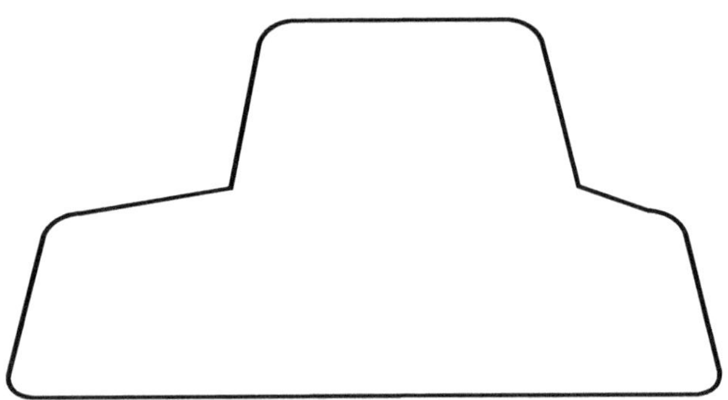

Step 2

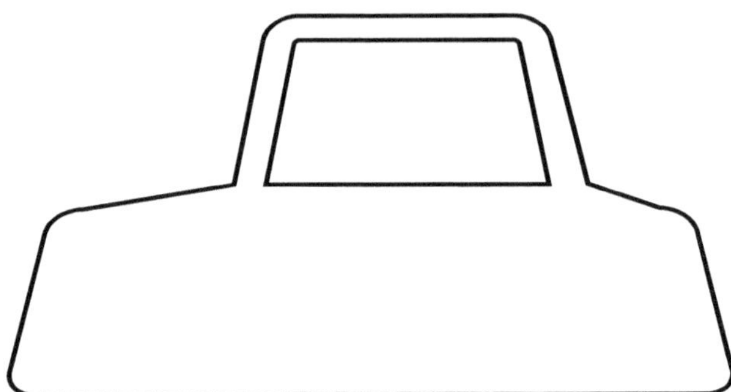

Step 3

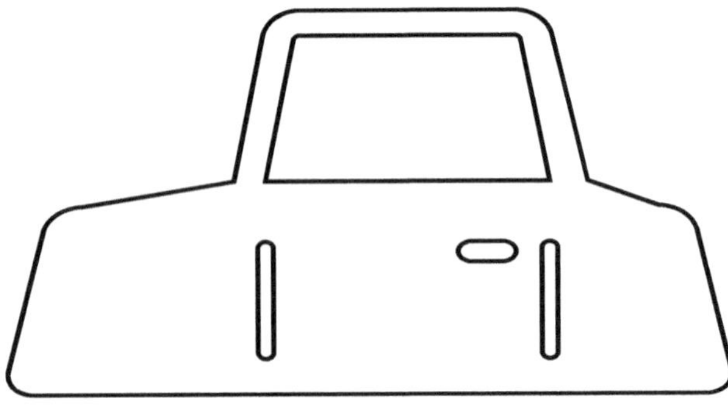

Step 4

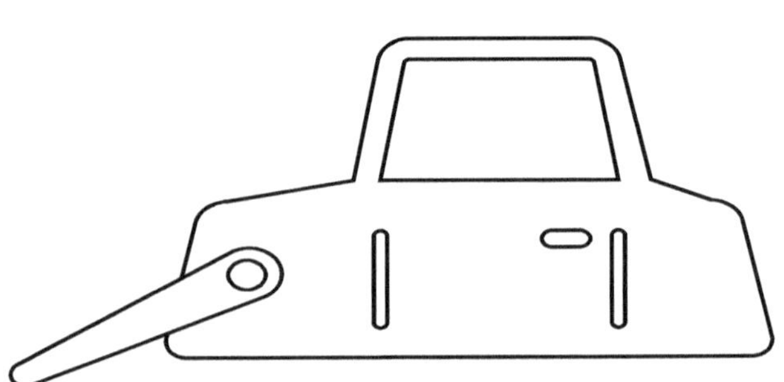

Step 5

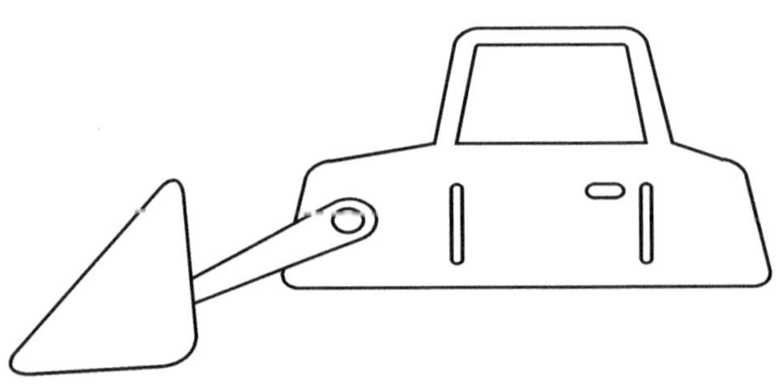

Step 6

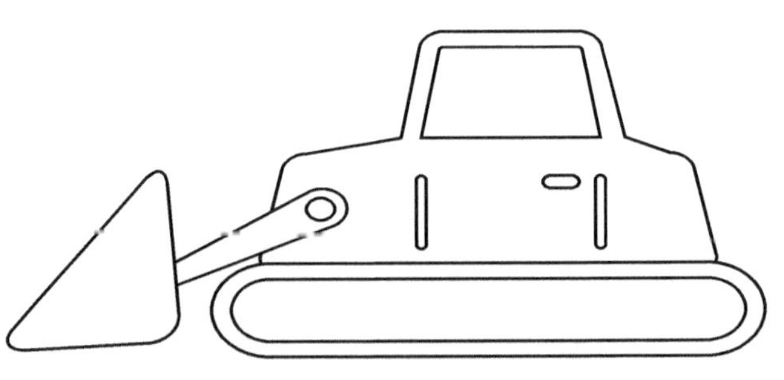

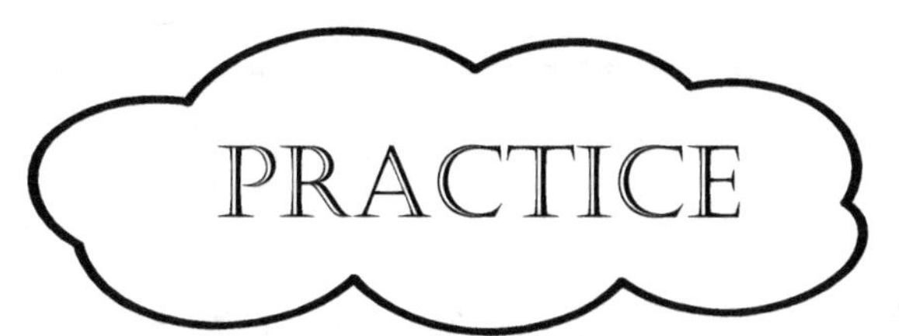
PRACTICE

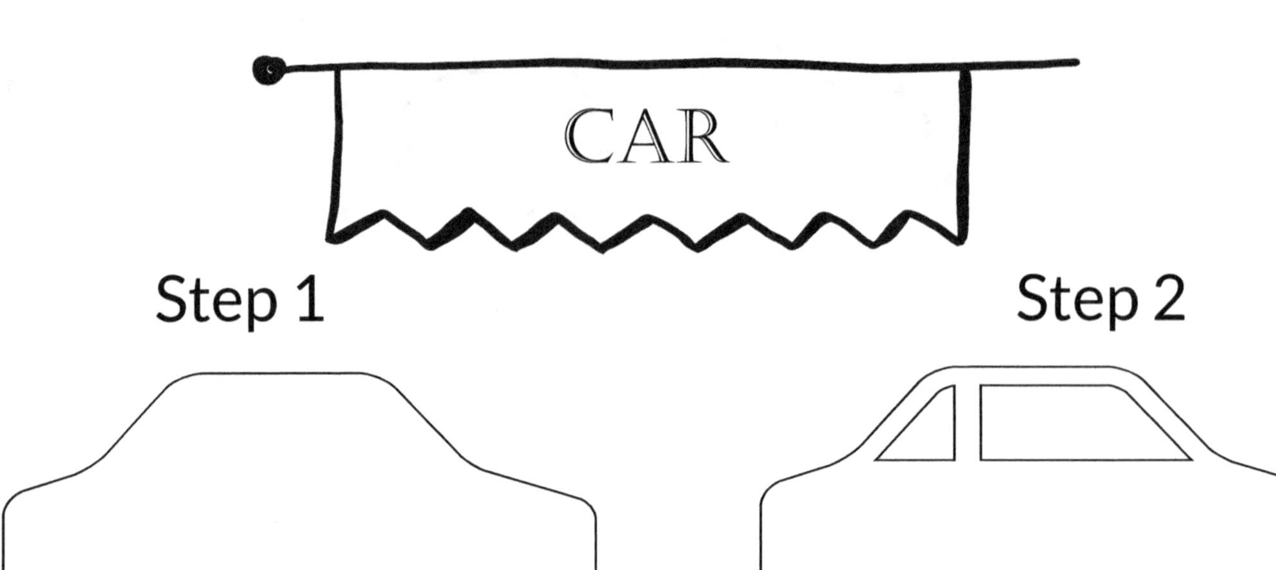

Step 3

Step 4

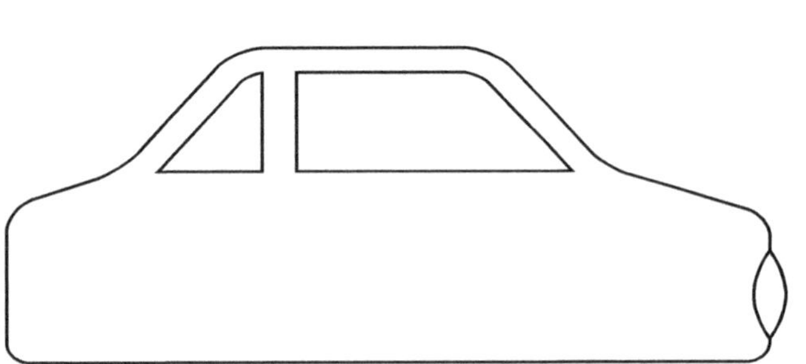

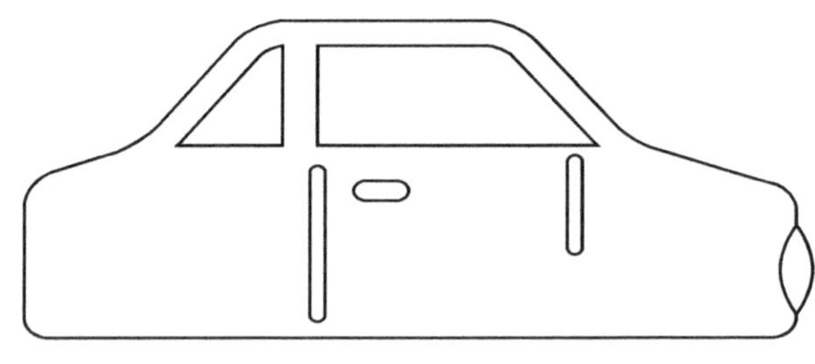

Step 5

Step 6

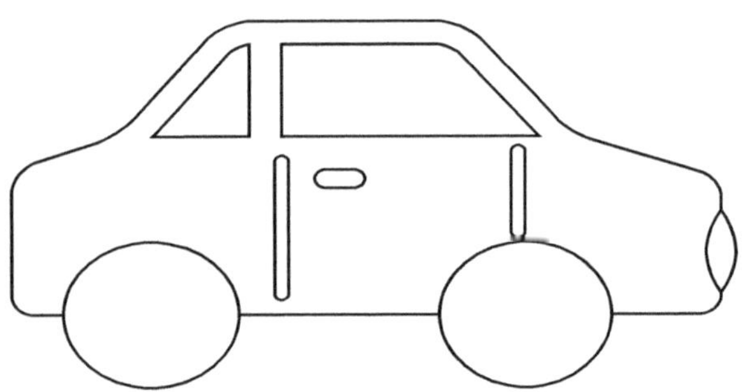

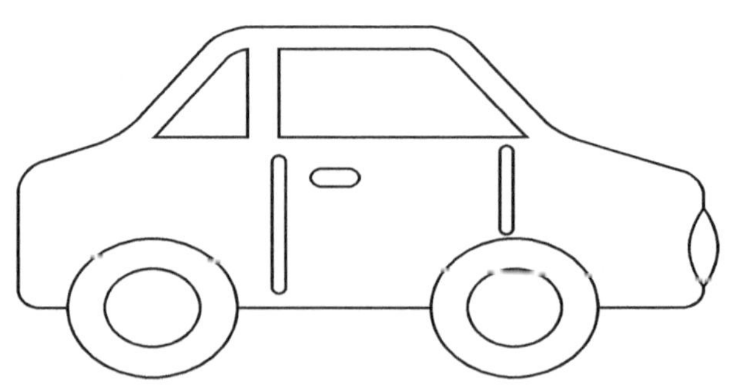

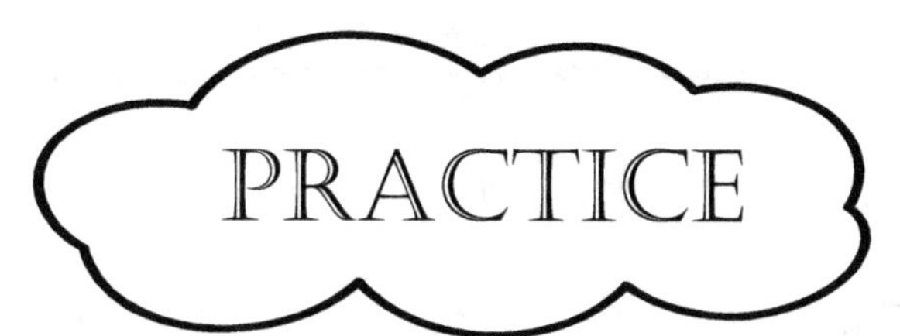
PRACTICE

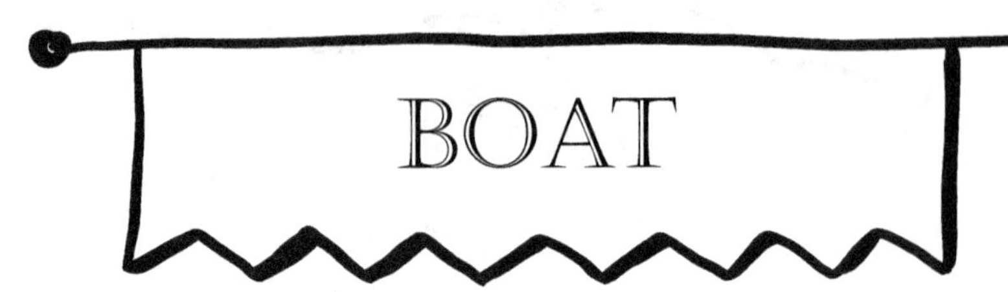

Step 1

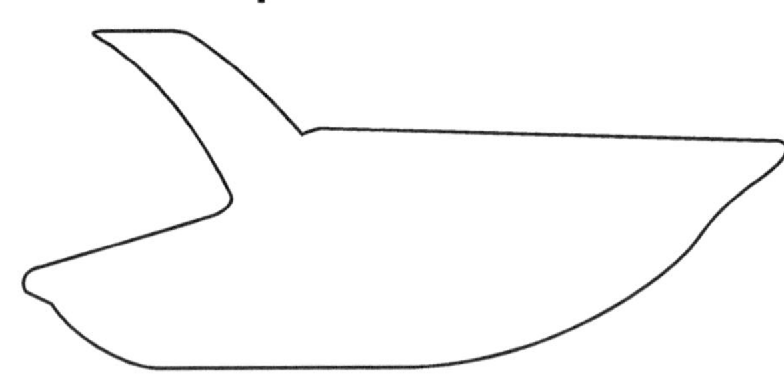

Step 2

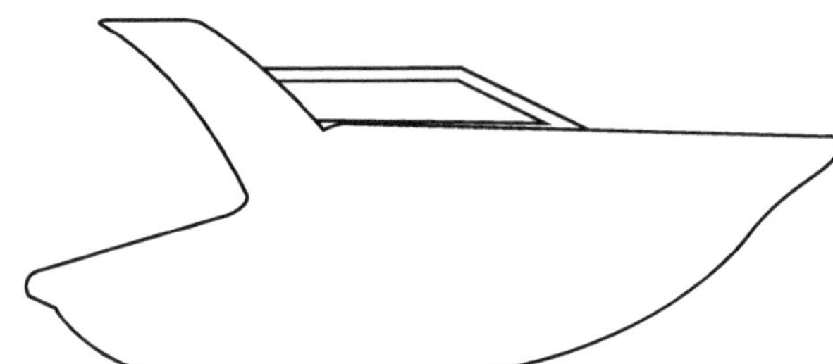

Step 3

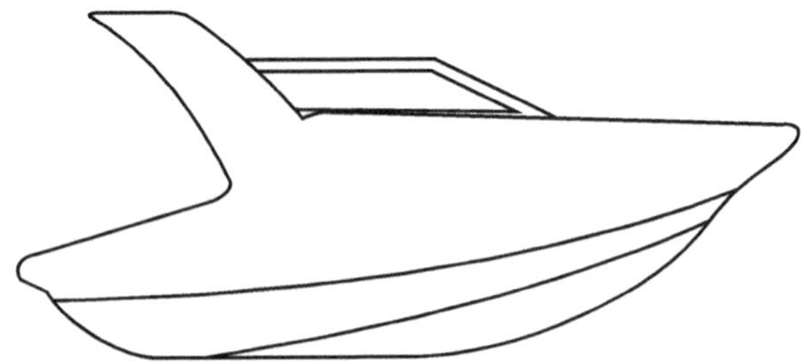

Step 4

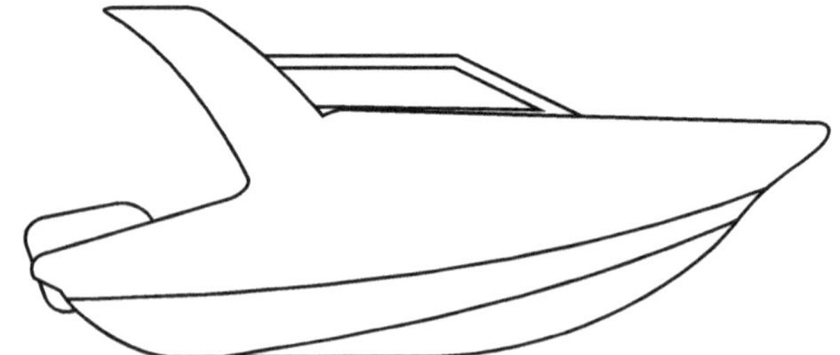

Step 5

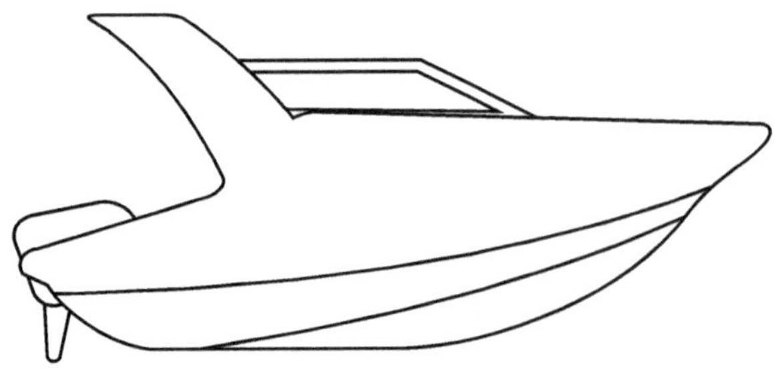

Step 6

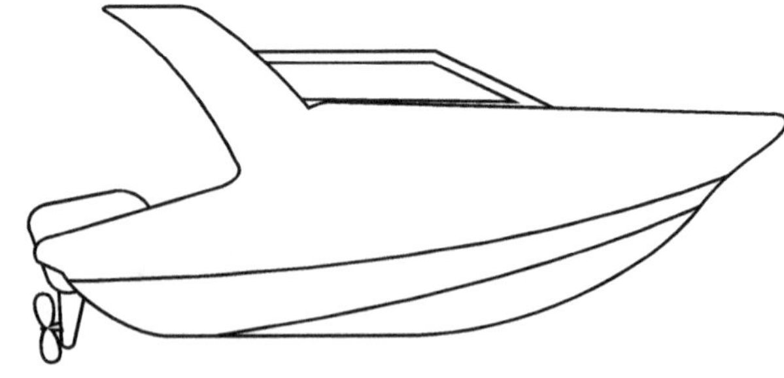

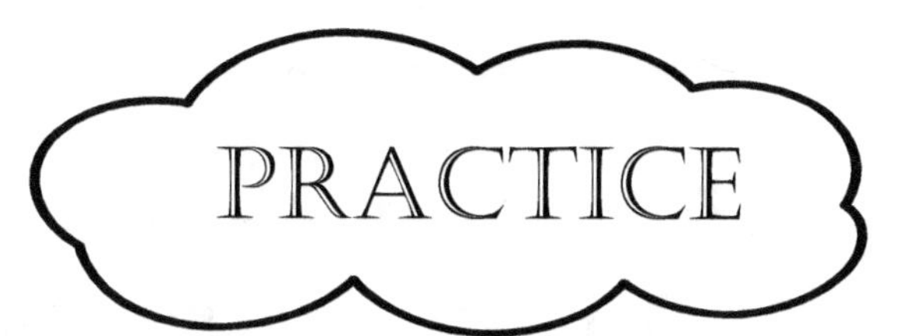
PRACTICE

SCOOTER

Step 1

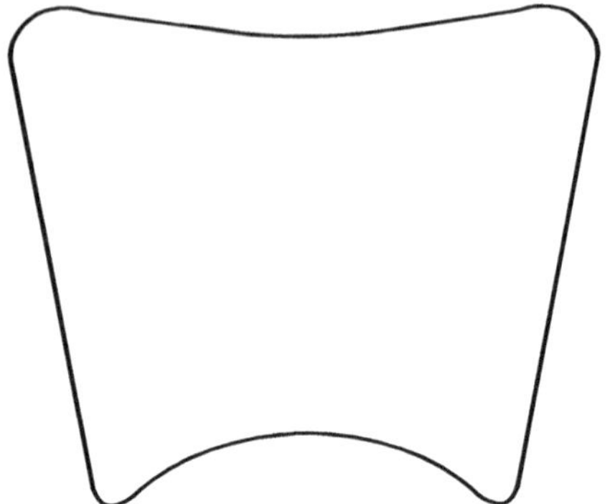

Step 2

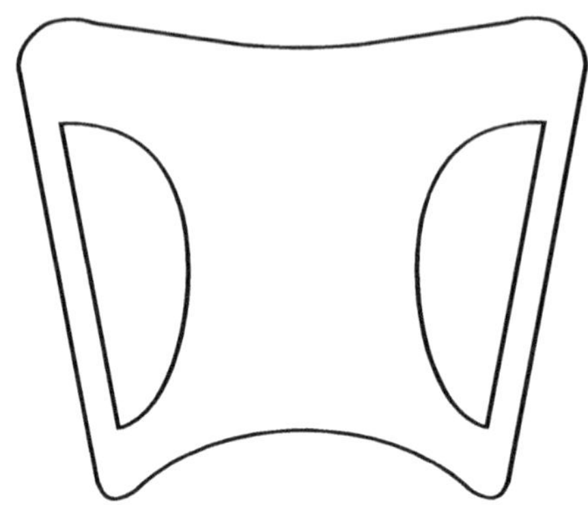

Step 3

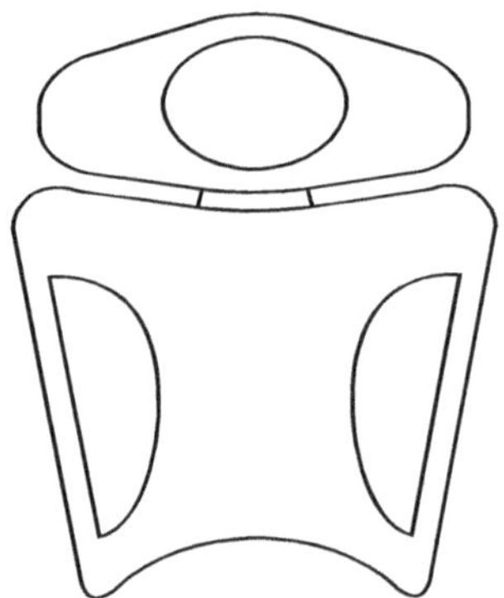

Step 4

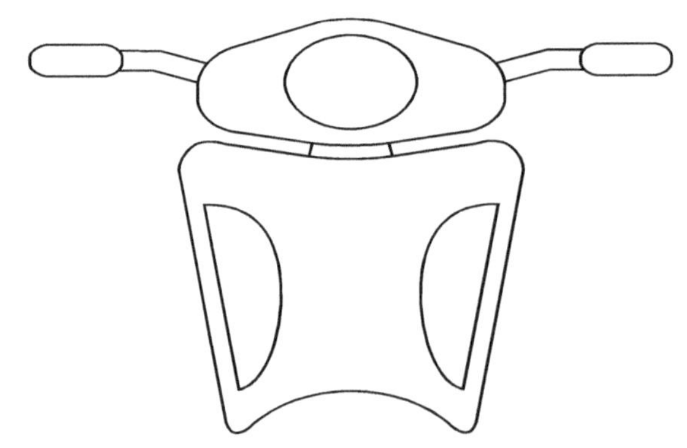

Step 5

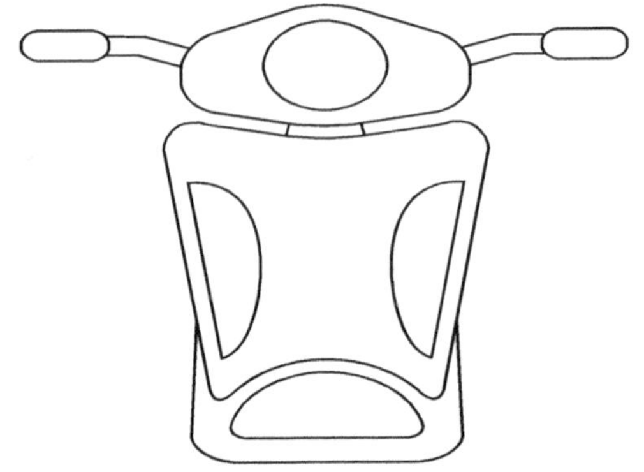

Step 6

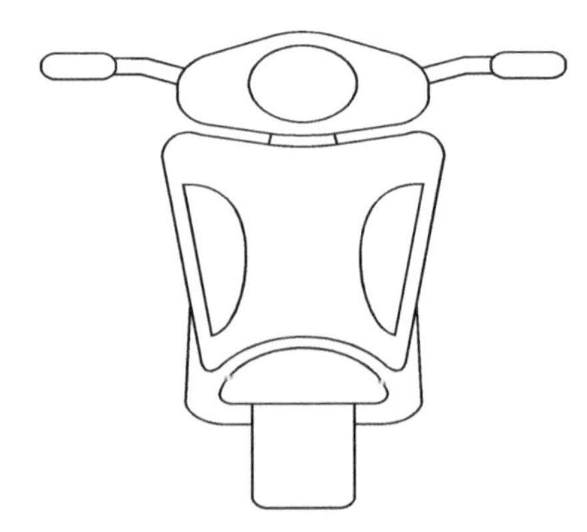

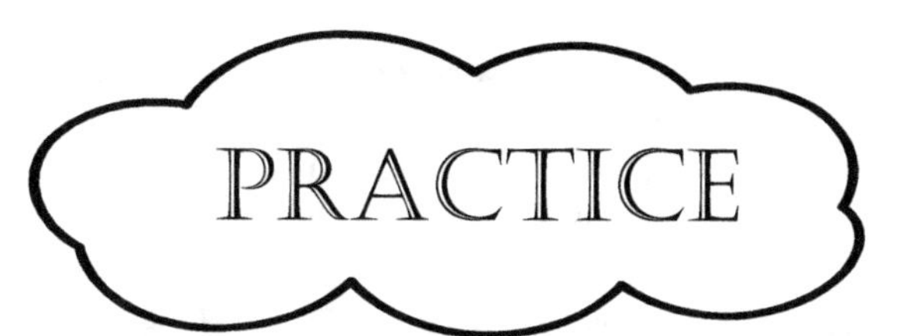
PRACTICE

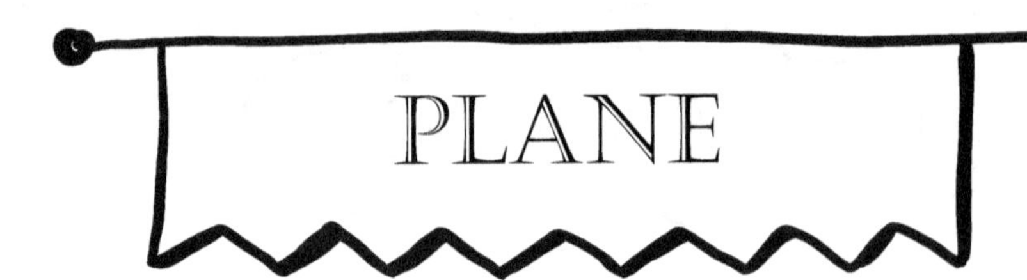

Step 1

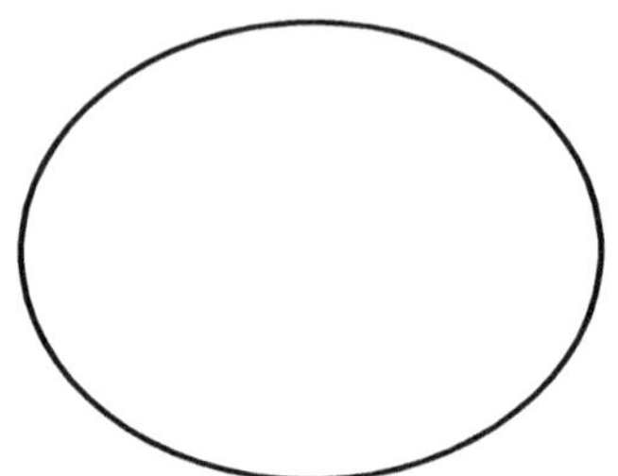

Step 2

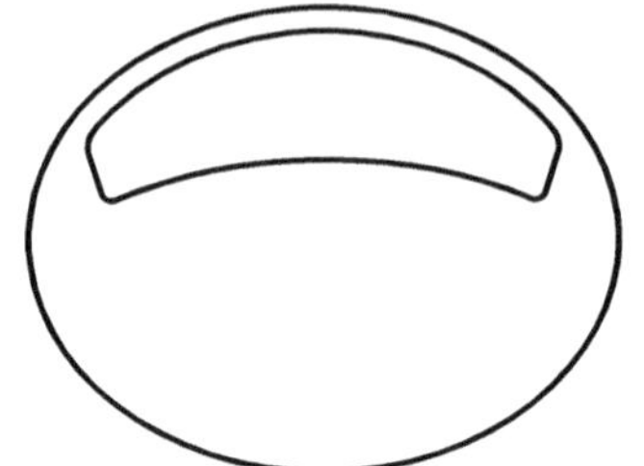

Step 3

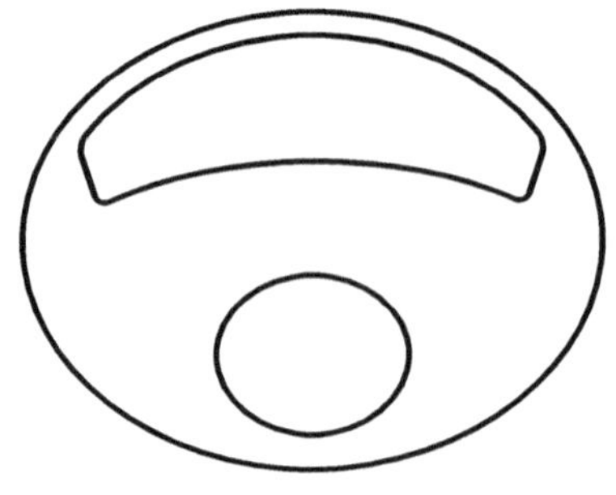

Step 4

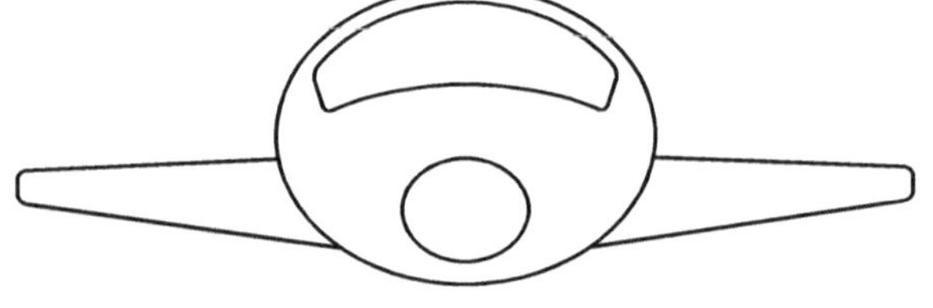

Step 5

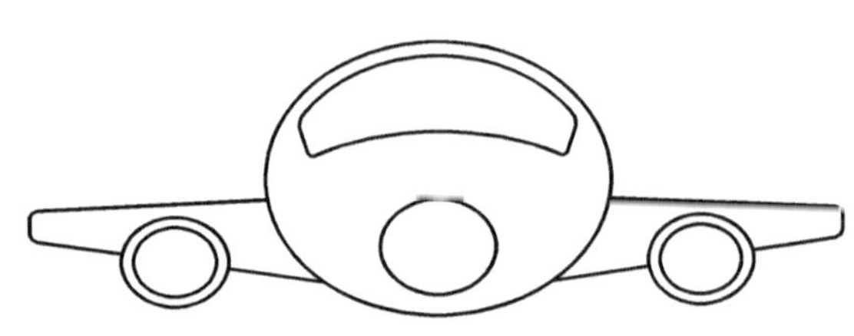

Step 6

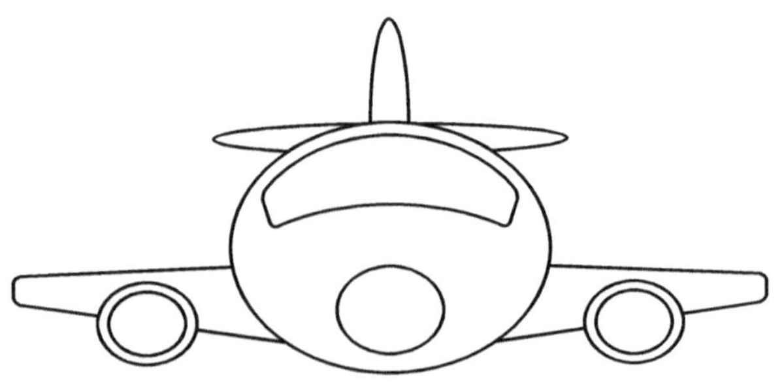

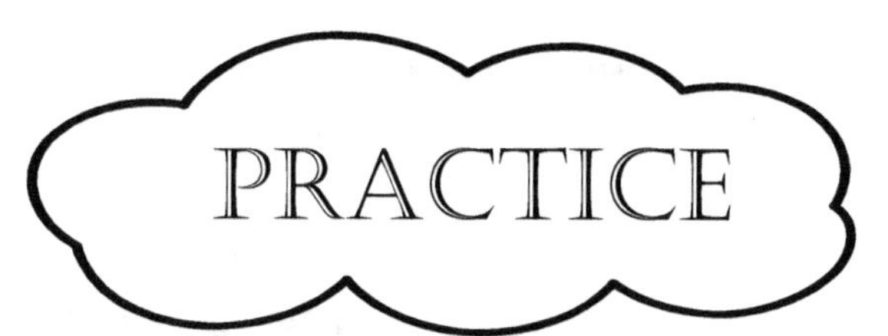
PRACTICE

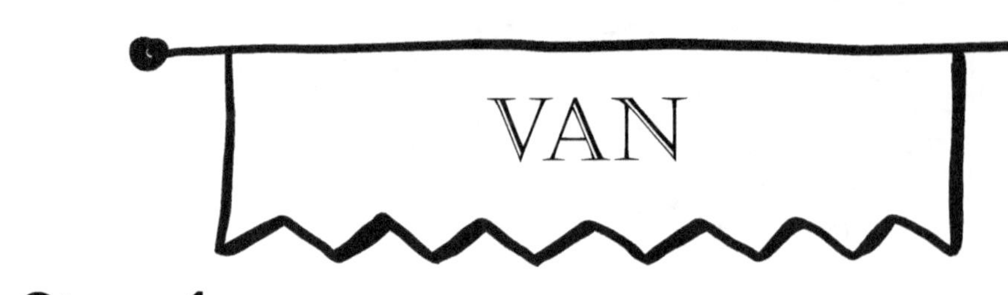

Step 1

Step 2

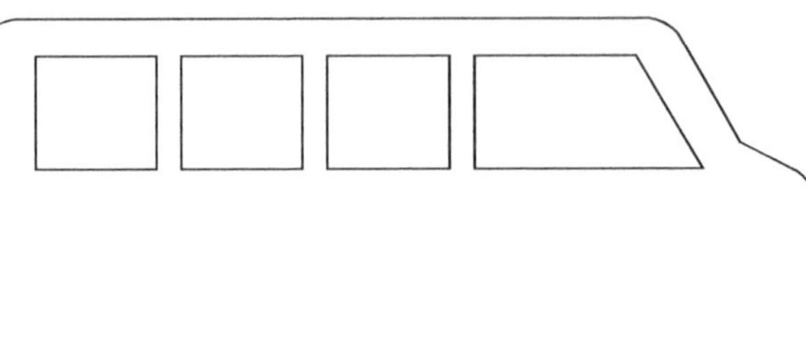

Step 3

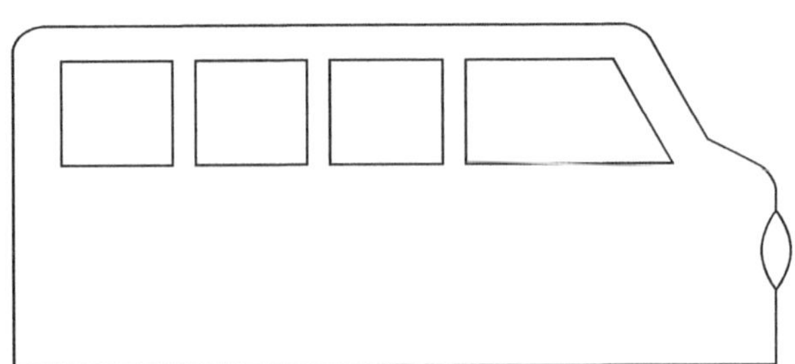

Step 4

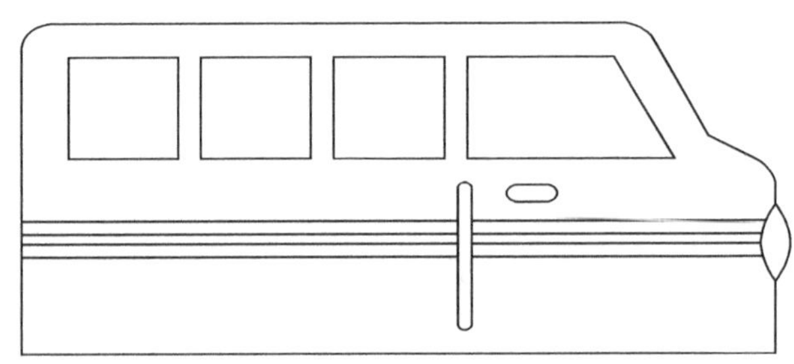

Step 5

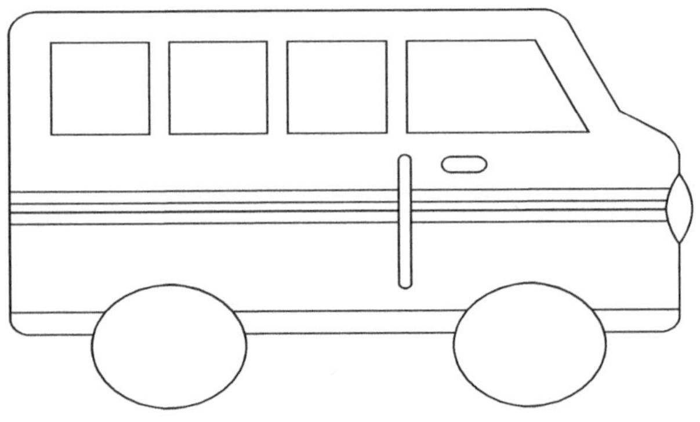

Step 6

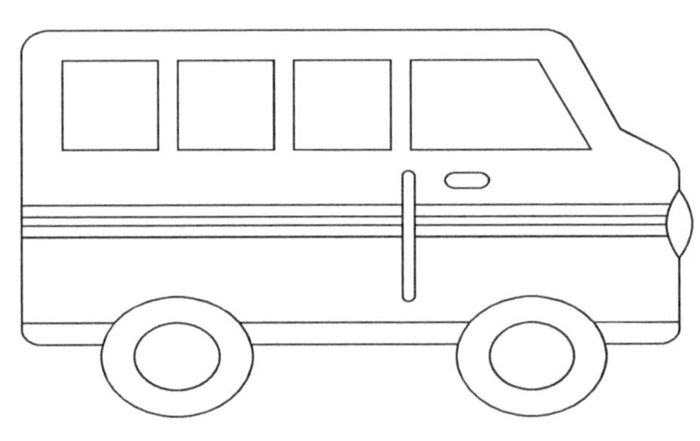

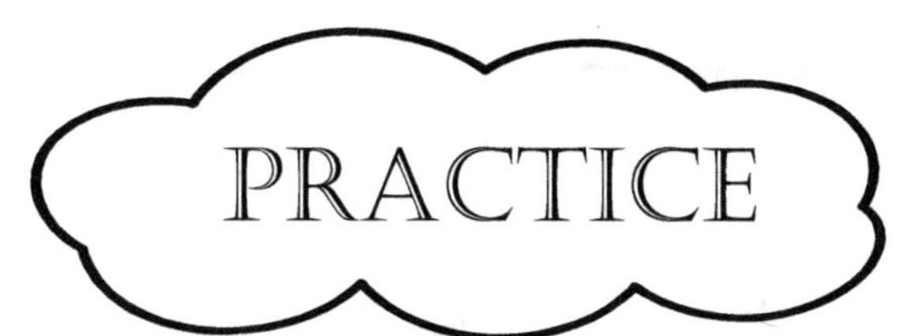
PRACTICE

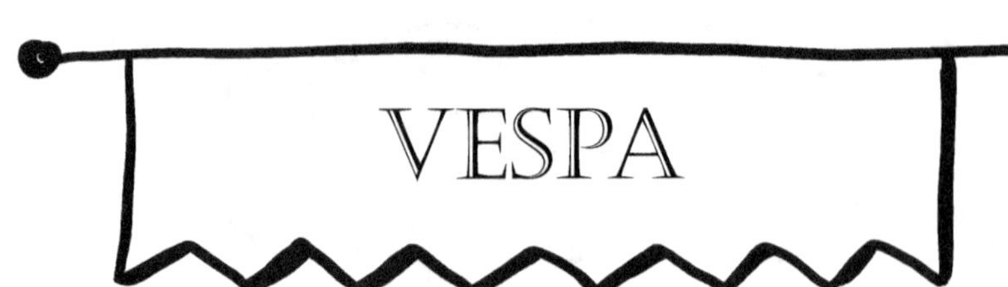

Step 1

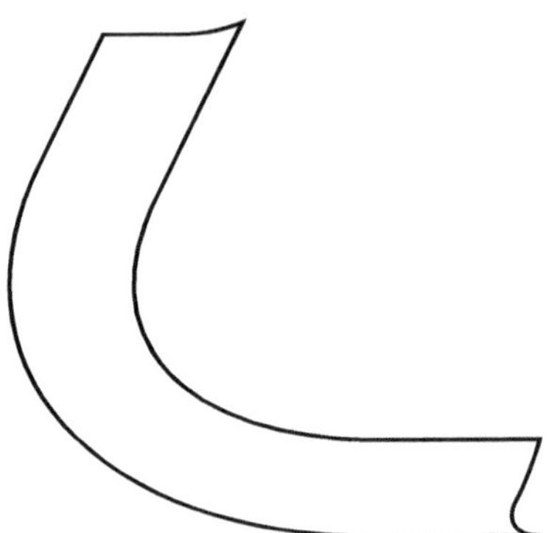

Step 2

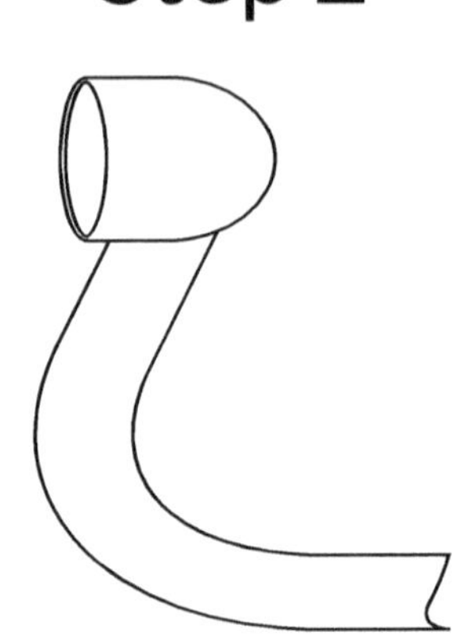

Step 3

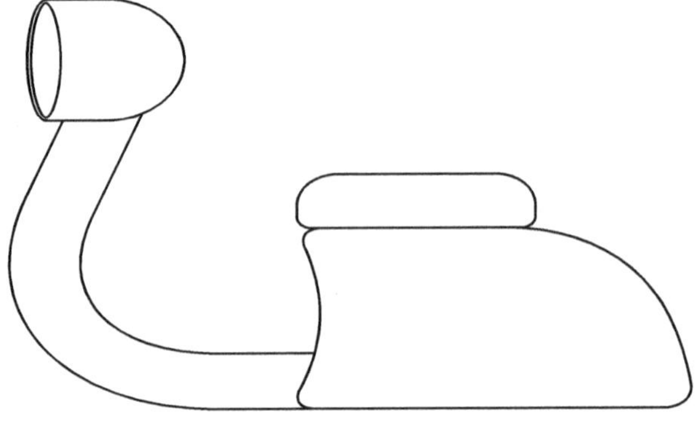

Step 4

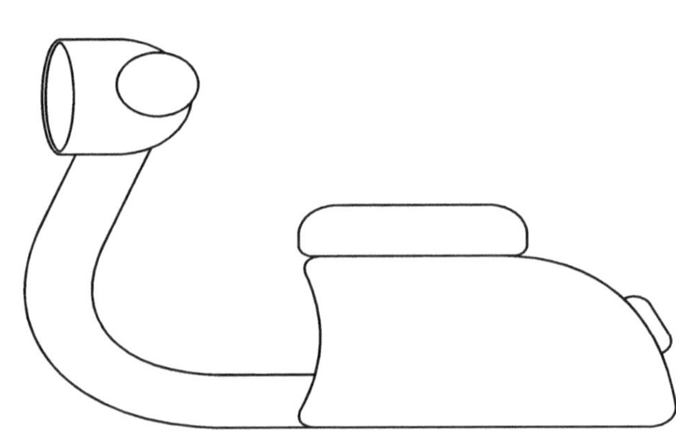

Step 5

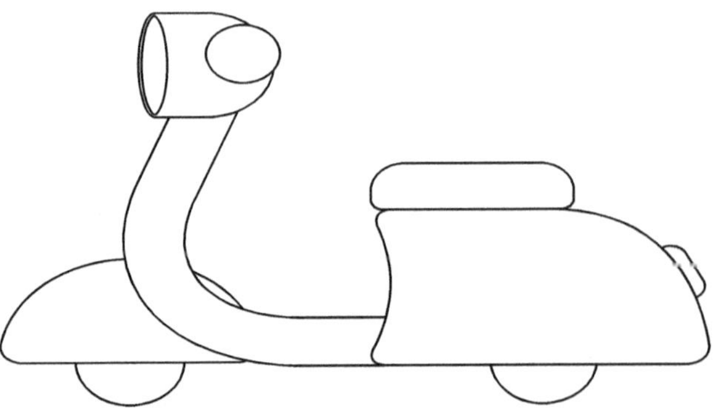

Step 6

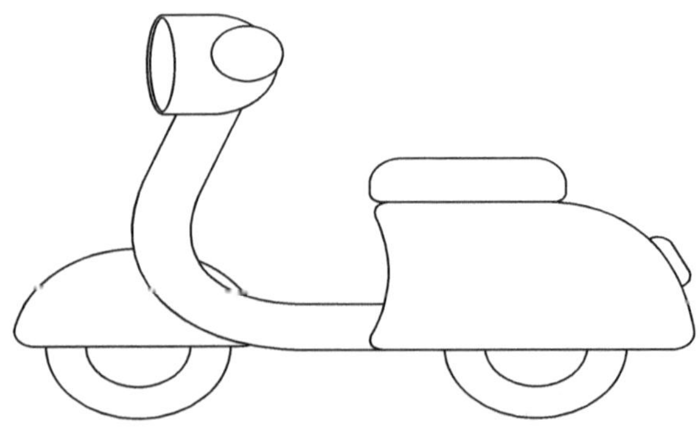

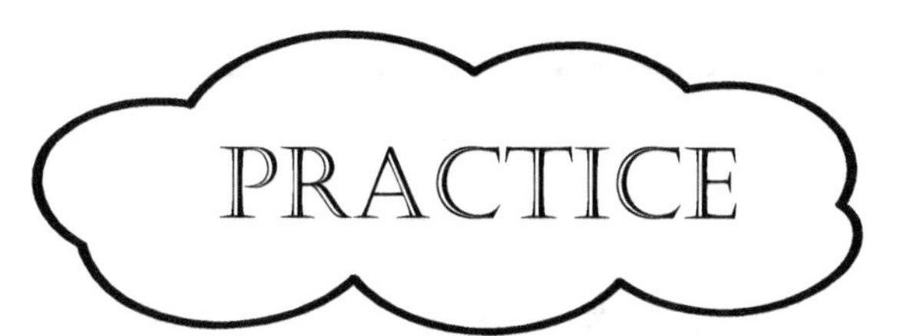
PRACTICE

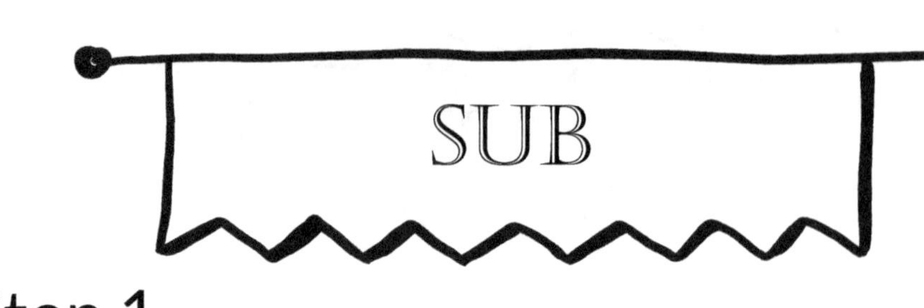

Step 1

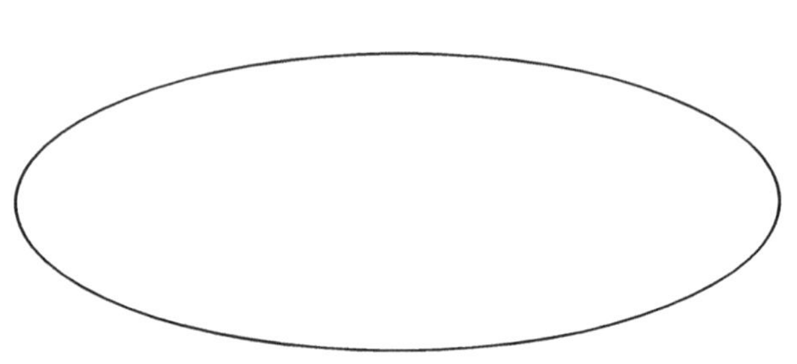

Step 2

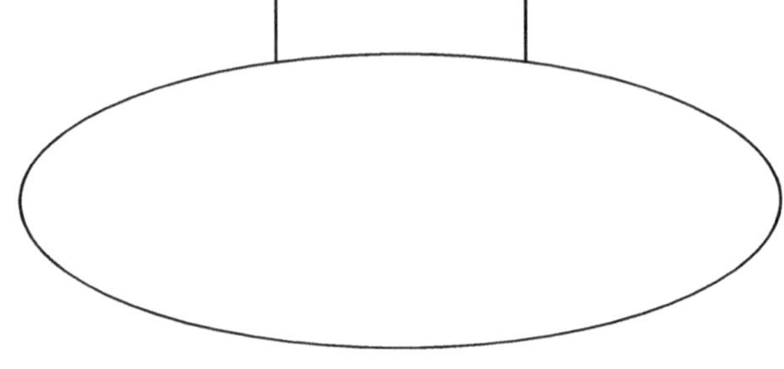

Step 3

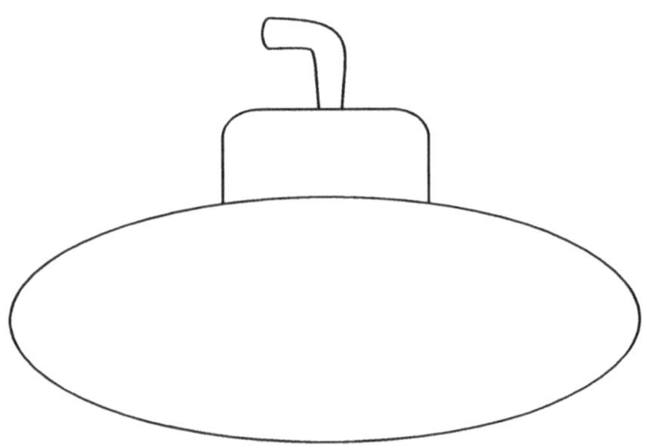

Step 4

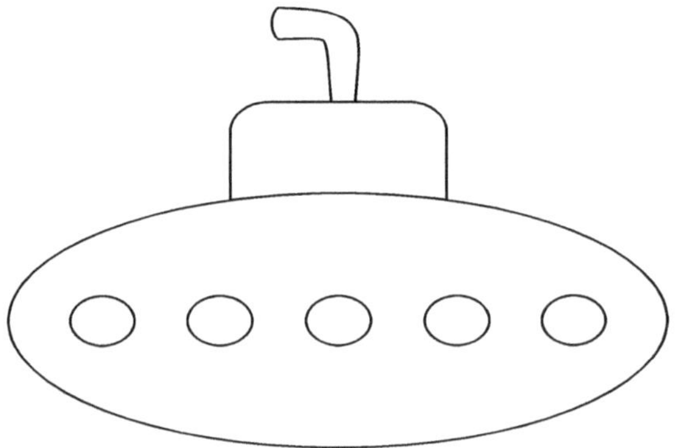

Step 5

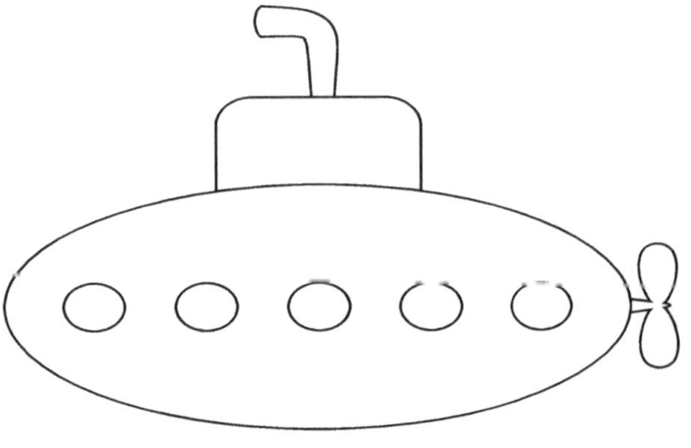

Step 6

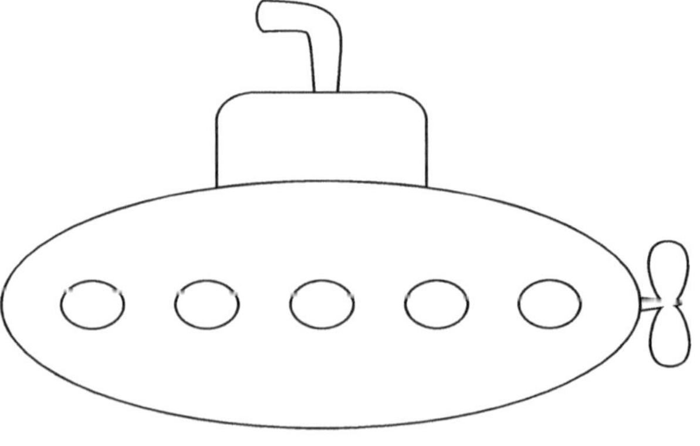

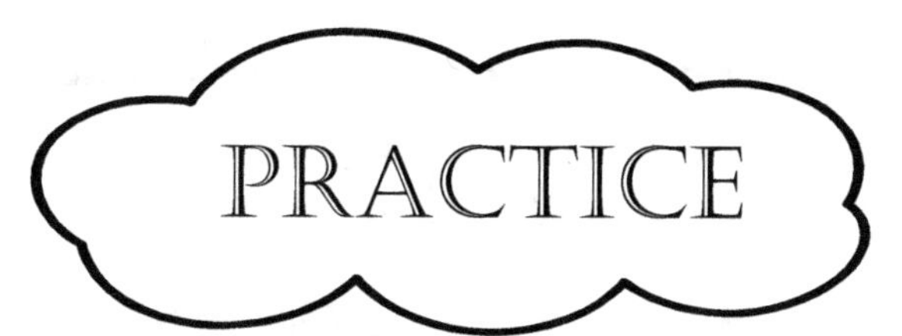
PRACTICE

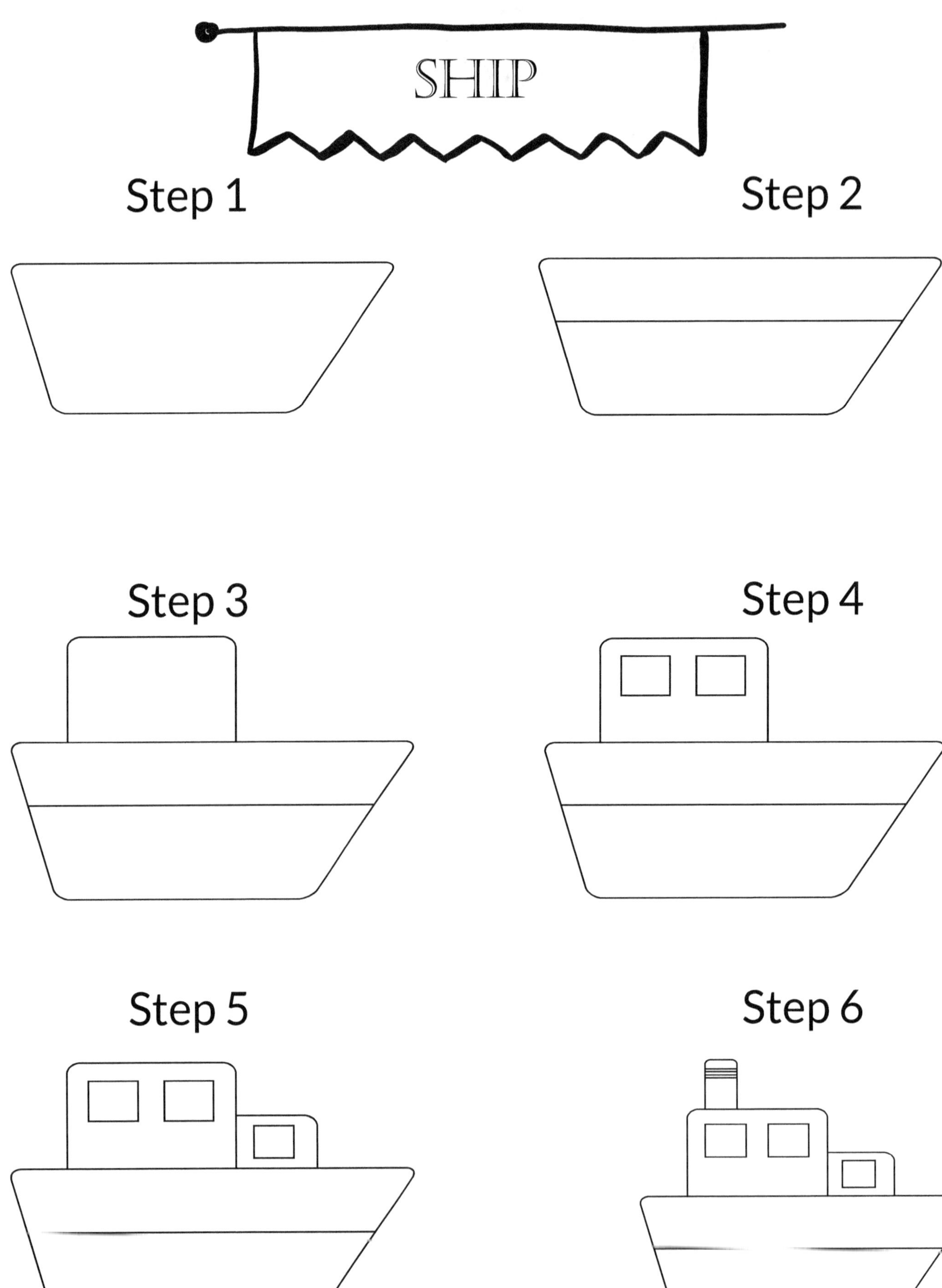
SHIP
Step 1
Step 2
Step 3
Step 4
Step 5
Step 6

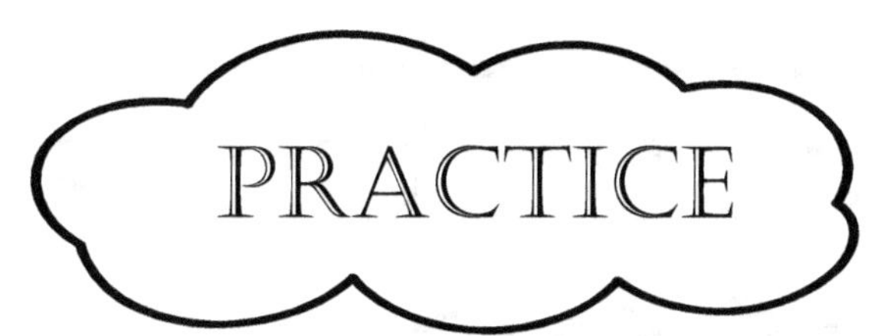
PRACTICE

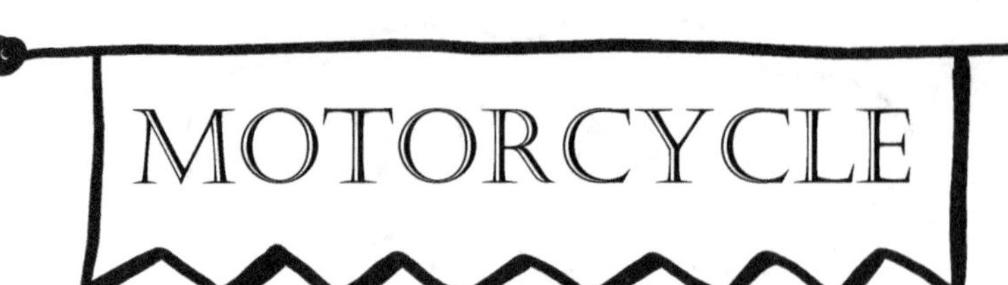

Step 1

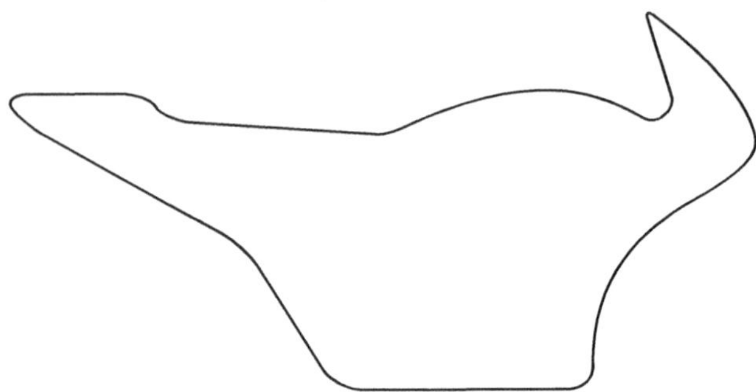

Step 2

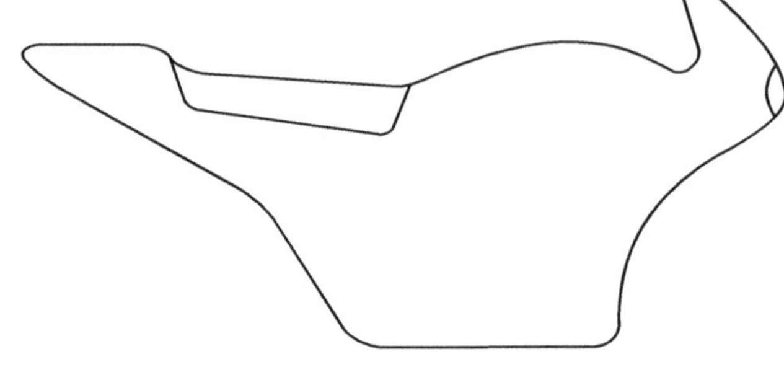

Step 3

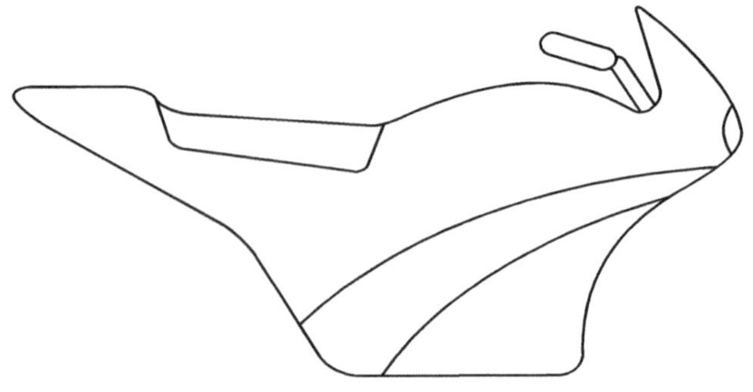

Step 4

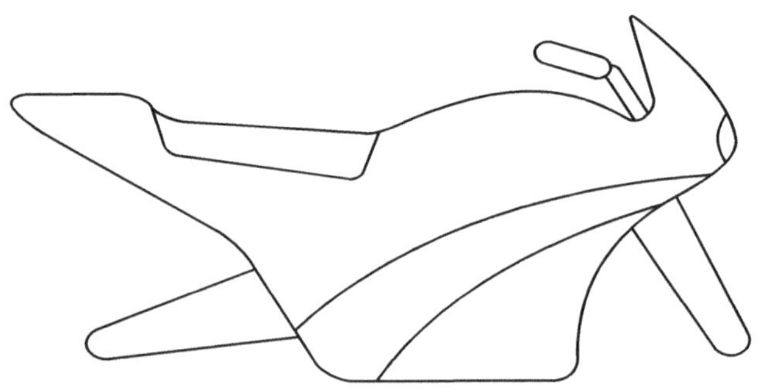

Step 5

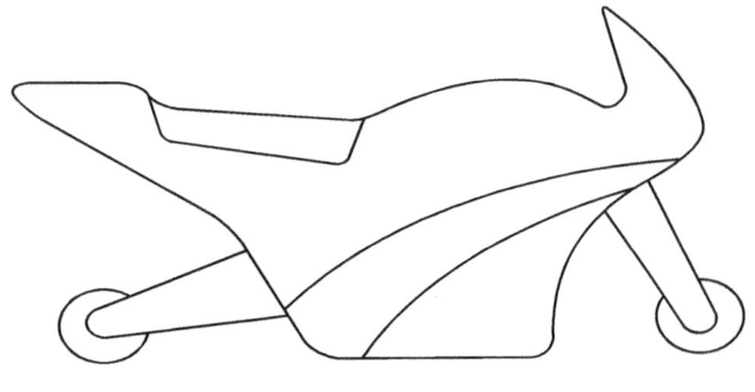

Step 6

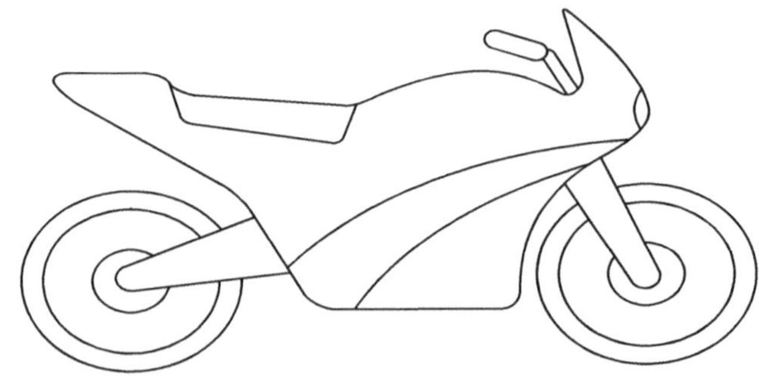

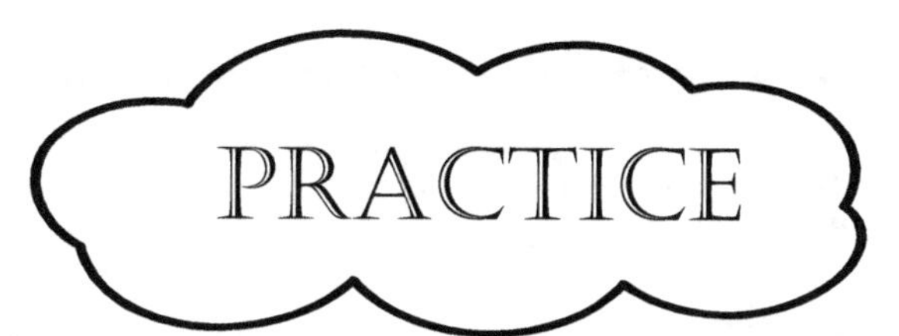
PRACTICE

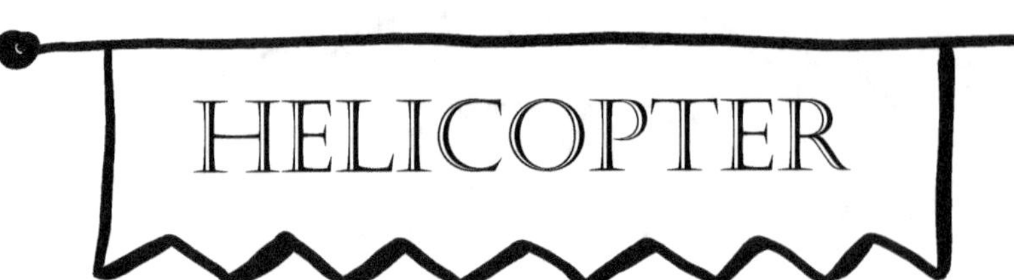

Step 1

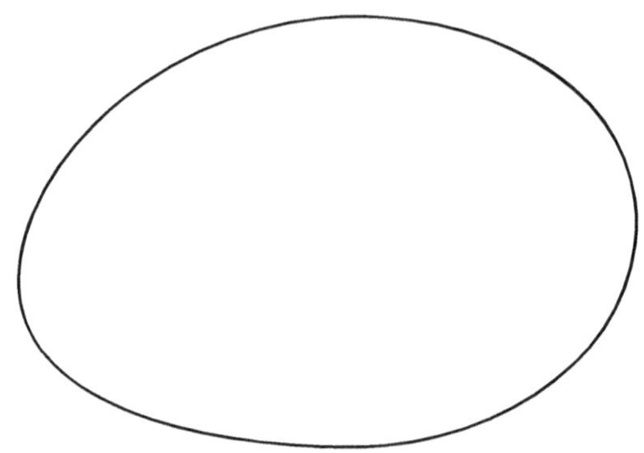

Step 2

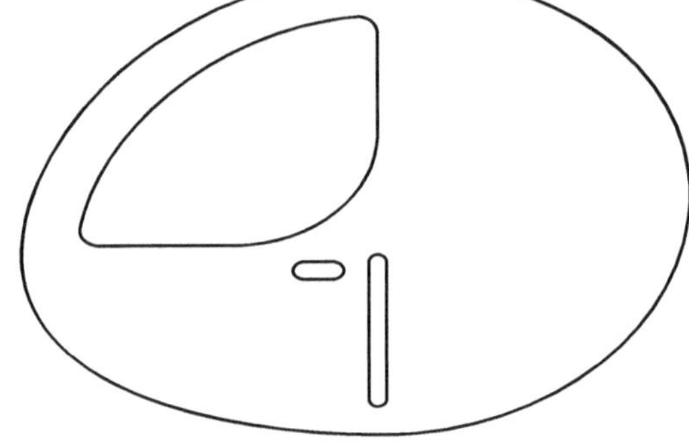

Step 3

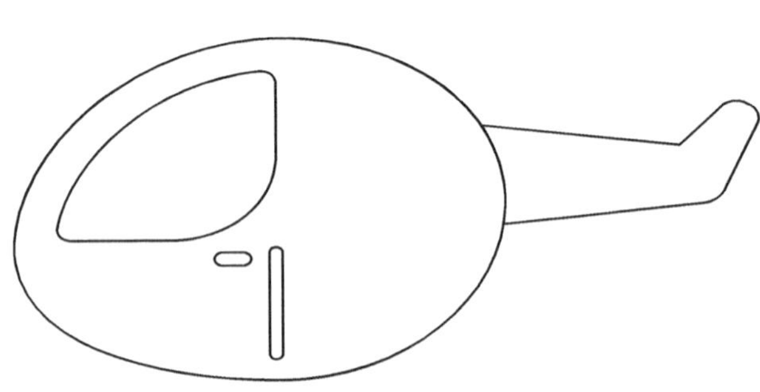

Step 4

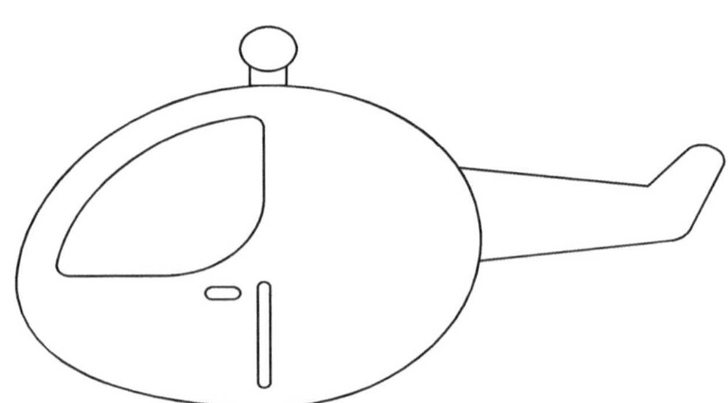

Step 5

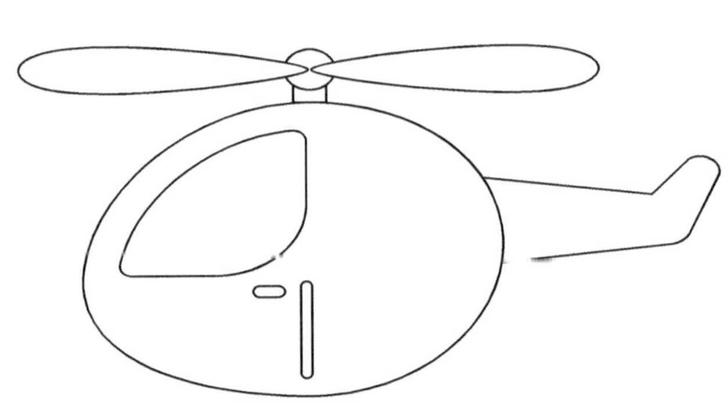

Step 6

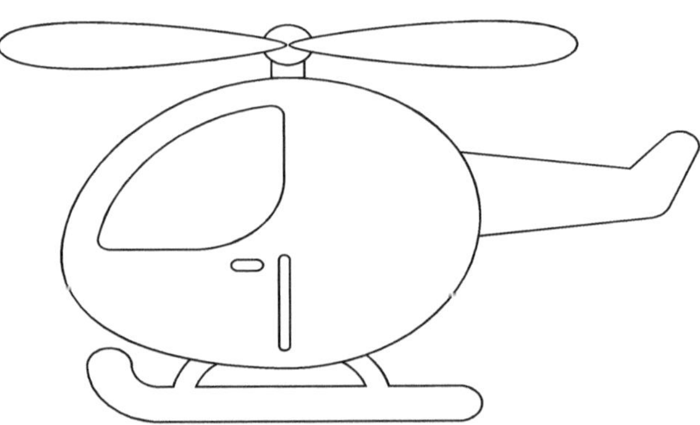

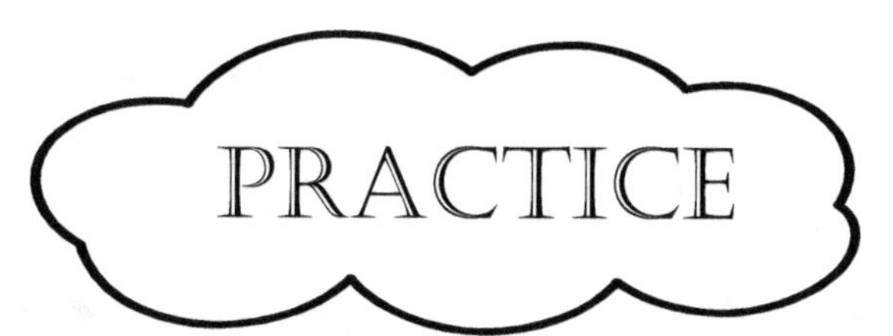
PRACTICE

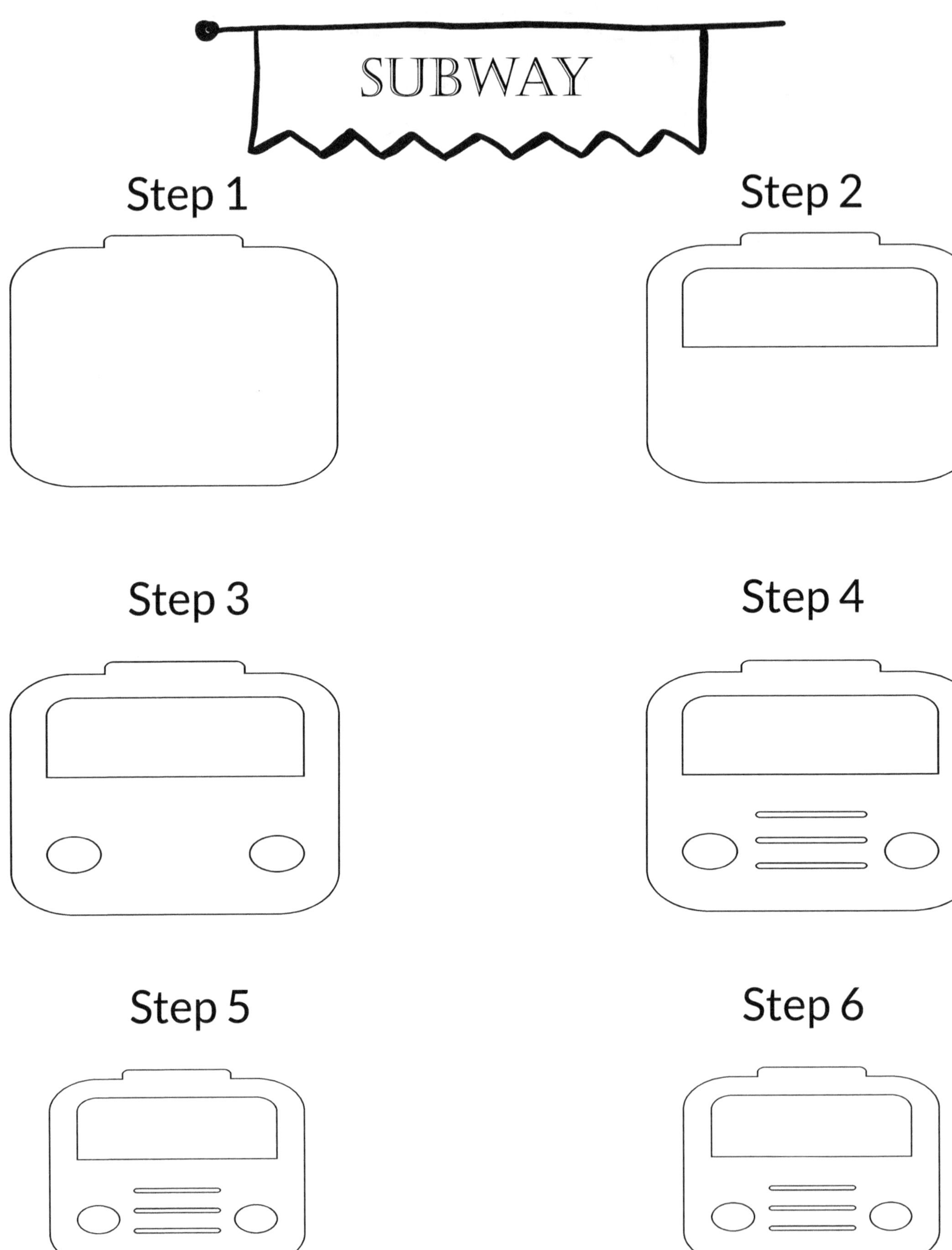
SUBWAY
Step 1
Step 2
Step 3
Step 4
Step 5
Step 6

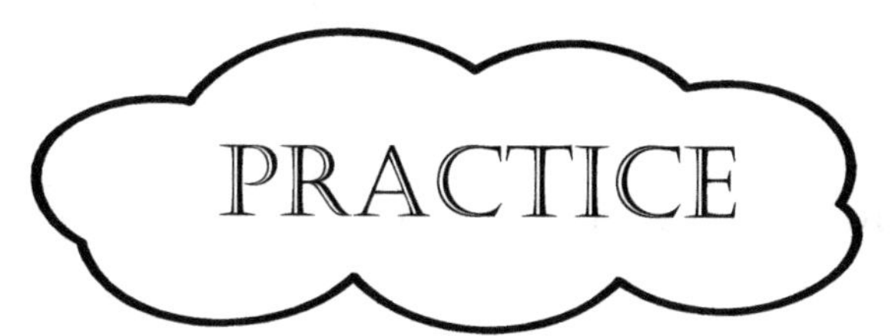
PRACTICE

Thank You for your purchase.

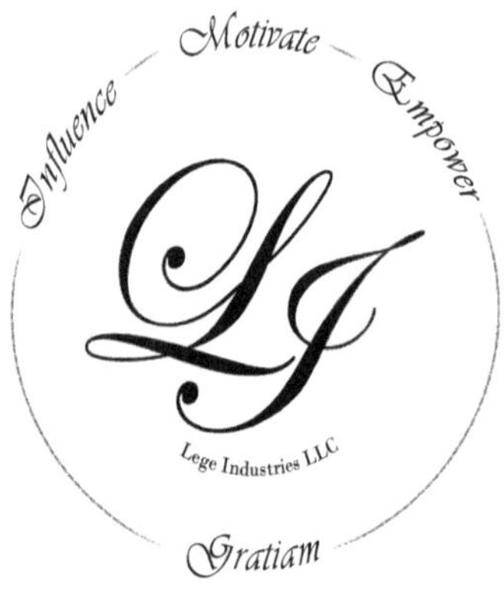

Check out other great books like this one by visiting us at:

https://legeindustriesllc.com

Or scanning the QR code below

www.ingramcontent.com/pod-product-compliance
Lightning Source LLC
LaVergne TN
LVHW080043170826
845677LV00024B/1563
9798987895771